# POPE
# JOHN PAUL II
---
# A TRIBUTE

Grange
BOOKS

# POPE
# JOHN PAUL II
## A TRIBUTE

Published 2005 by Grange Books
an imprint of Grange Books PLC.
The Grange
Kings North Industrial Estate
Hoo nr. Rochester
Kent, UK
ME3 9ND

www.grangebooks.co.uk

All enquiries please email info@grangebooks.co.uk

All notations of errors or omissions and other correspondence (author inquiries, permissions) concerning the content of this book should be addressed to:
TAJ Books, 27 Ferndown Gardens, Cobham, Surrey, UK, KT11 2BH
info@tajbooks.com
www.tajbooks.com

ISBN 1-84013-857-2

Printed in China
1 2 3 4 5 09 08 07 06 05

# Contents

## POPE JOHN PAUL II

On April 3, 2005, Pope John Paul II died peacefully in his sleep in his private apartments in the Vatican. He had received the Last Rites and was ready to meet his maker. He had been the Supreme Pontiff for 26 years, the longest serving pope in modern times and the first non-Italian for 455 years. His reign has been widely acclaimed as being responsible for stabilizing the Roman Catholic Church, showing a strong religious lead in a rapidly declining moral atmosphere, and for re-establishing the word of God in Africa and South America in particular.

John Paul II became pope at the comparatively young age of 58 and brought with him a youthful, Polish vigor previously unknown in the Vatican. When he arrived in October 1978 he was an unknown quantity to the vast majority of Roman Catholics around the world; by the time he died had become a much admired and loved holy figure, even beyond the confines of the Catholic Church. He had met in person and been seen in the flesh by more people around the world than any other pope, in over 100 international journeys. He used his position and charisma not only for the good of the church, in particular in fighting for the rights of the poor and underprivileged, but also to speak both publicly and privately to political leaders—he was unafraid to point out their shortcomings and embarrass them into behaving better, even in front of their own countries.

Pope John Paul II was born as Karel Józef Wojtyla in Wadowice in southern Poland on May 18, 1920. His mother was Emilia Kaczorowska and his father, also named Karel, was formerly an officer in the Austro-Hungarian Army and a deeply religious man. Tragically his mother died in 1929 of congenital heart disease and kidney failure when Lolek (Karel's childhood nickname) was only nine years old. A few years later, his brother Edmund —a doctor—caught scarlet fever from a patient and died in 1932 at the age of only 26. So, Karel was brought up on his own by his devout father who emphasized to his young son the importance of study and prayer. In his free time Karel visited the Wadowice Jewish community where he had many friends. This was to provide him with a particular understanding of and sympathy for the Jewish faith.

After graduating from Marcin Wadowita high school in Wadowice in summer 1938, father and son moved to Kraków so that in the fall Karel could attend Jagiellonian University to study Polish language and literature, philosophy, Russian, and Old Church Slavonic. He also joined a local dramatic society where he reveled in performing, an enthusiasm that he kept all his life. For a time Karel even had thoughts of becoming an actor. At university he found time to work as a volunteer librarian but he also did compulsory military training in the Acedemic Legion. Amazingly, he also managed to study French in his private time.

At the outbreak of World War II in September 1939 Poland was occupied by German forces. To escape the Nazi occupation Karel and his father joined hundreds of fleeing refugees streaming eastward, but after walking 120 miles they heard of the Russian invasion of Poland and reluctantly turned back to Kraków. The university was immediately closed by the new authorities and Karel took work as a restaurant messenger while he quietly allied himself with the Polish resistance. He did this for a year while continuing his education, in particular learning French, in secret. Then, in fall 1940 he took work in a limestone quarry working as a manual laborer. The work was hard but the pay was good and it allowed him to study theology in secret. Just as importantly, it exempted him from serving in the armed forces. During this period his father died (in 1941), leaving Karel without immediate family.

In 1942 Karel joined the underground seminary in Kraków run by Cardinal Adam Stefan Sapieha, the Archbishop of Kraków, where he studied theology. He knew that this would have been his father's wish and by then he was starting to understand that his true vocation lay with the church.

Then, one day on February 29, 1944, while walking home after completing a day's work at the quarry, Karel was knocked over by a German truck. As well as being knocked unconscious, he was badly cut and his shoulder severely damaged. He had been extremely lucky not to have been killed; instead he was taken to hospital where he remained for two weeks suffering the painful after effects, in particular severe concussion. The accident and his miraculous survival conclusively proved to Karel his priestly vocation and from then on his path through life was clear to him.

Six months later, in August 1944, the Warsaw Uprising began. To stop the same sort of insurgency in Kraków, the Gestapo rounded up all young men on August 6—Black Sunday. They searched Karel Wojtyla's house but he managed to hide away until he could escape to the archbishop's residence where he stayed out the war. At last, on the night of January 17, 1945, the Nazis left Kraków and Karel was able to return to university and his studies. By the end of the war Poland had fallen under the political control of the Soviet Union and the country came under a severely Communist regime not sympathetic to Roman Catholicism, or indeed any religion, but Karel was able to continue his studies and graduated with distinction.

November 1, 1946, was a momentous day for Karel Wojtyla because it was the day that he was ordained as a priest by his protector Cardinal Sapieha. He was sent straight to the Angelicum (the Pontifical Athenaeum of St Thomas Aquinas) in Rome to study. For his doctorate Karel explored how St. John of the Cross understood his faith in a very personal way, in a fashion that also had immense appeal for him, too. On completion of his thesis in summer 1948, Karel returned to his homeland where he took up his first pastoral assignment at the little village of Niegowic, 15 miles from Kraków. While there he continued to write doctrinal texts and encourage religious freedom, but within a few months (March 1949) he was transferred to a parish in Kraków itself, St. Florians. In addition Karel resumed his connection with Jagiellonian University where he taught ethics; at this he was so successful that he was invited to become a professor of ethics at the Catholic University of Lublin. His texts and doctrinal papers were widely read within the church and particularly appreciated by Pope Paul VI; this, together with his reputation for fighting for the freedom of the Catholic church despite the restrictions of the Communist regime, meant that he caught the eye of the church hierarchy.

With such a significant reputation Karel was obviously destined for greater things and in 1958 he was elevated to the position of auxiliary Bishop of Kraków. Then, after four busy years, Karel Wojtyla became Bishop of Kraków at the age of 38. This important post made him one of the highest ranking clergymen in Poland. As such he was invited to contribute to the Second Vatican Council which started in June 1963. The Council had been called as Pope John XXIII said, "to renew ourselves and the flocks committed to us, so that there may

radiate before all men the loveable features of Jesus Christ, who shines in our hearts that God's splendor may be revealed." During these proceedings, in December 30, 1963, Karel was promoted when the new pope, Paul VI, appointed him Archbishop of Kraków.

After four sessions the Second Vatican Council closed on December 8, 1965. The sessions produced 16 documents and Archbishop Wojtyla made vital contributions to two of the most important: Dignitatis Humanae and Gaudium et Spes ("Decree on Religious Freedom" and "Pastoral Constitution on the Church in the Modern World" respectively). These emphasized that the church must be a worshipping and serving community open to different ways of seeing God but also flexible with its point of view and religious traditions. The most obvious result for most Catholics was that the Mass was celebrated in their own native language instead of Latin and the church also had a perceptibly friendlier, more open attitude towards non-Catholics.

Pope Paul VI was hugely impressed by Archbishop Wojtyla's ministry, and made him a cardinal on June 26, 1967; Karel Wojtila was still only 47 years old. Throughout this period in Poland Archbishop Wojtila was a continuous thorn in the Communist authorities' side as he agitated for greater religious freedoms for his flock. In August 1978 Pope Paul VI died. Archbishop Wojtyla journeyed to Rome to join the Papal Conclave in the Vatican City. After due consideration the 65-year old Albino Luciani, Cardinal Patriarch of Venice, was elected to the Papal See. He took the name Pope John Paul I in acknowledgement of his two illustrious predecessors. However, on September 28—after only 33 days as Pope—John Paul I was discovered dead in his Papal apartments.

Along with the other shocked papal delegates Archbishop Wojtyla returned to the Vatican in October 1978 to choose another pope. The contest was always going to be fraught as two particularly strong and well supported candidates were the front runners—the Archbishop of Florence, Giovanni Cardinal Benelli, and the Archbishop of Genoa, Giuseppe Cardinal Siri. The former was only a few votes short of election in the early ballots but could not conclude the voting. Finally, Archbishop Wojtyla was turned to as a compromise candidate and at the eighth and final ballot on October 21, 1978, the white smoke from the Vatican informed the waiting crowd that a new pope had been chosen. To many people's surprise Archbishop Wojtyla won sufficient votes to make him the 264th pope. He was the first non-Italian pope in 455 years (since the Dutch Hadrian VI, 1522–23) and at only 58 was the youngest pope since Pius IX in 1846. His Polish homeland was estatic at his election, particularly as the Communists seemingly still held unbreakable power there.

It was announced that Archbishop Wojtyla would take the name Pope John Paul II in reference to his predecessors. The following day he celebrated Mass in the Sistine Chapel and delivered his first blessing to the world as pope, *Urbi et Orbi*. It was broadcast around the world on the radio.

On May 13, 1981, Pope John Paul II firmly believed he was the beneficiary of a miracle sanctioned by the Virgin Mary who intervened to save his life. That day when he entered St Peter's Square to address an audience, he was the victim of an assassination attempt. Mehmet al-Agca, a Turkish gunman, shot him in front of a stunned crowd. Whisked off to hospital, Pope John Paul II needed virtually an entire blood transfusion; his injuries were so severe that he was given the Last Rites as he hovered between life and death. It took John Paul a long time to recover from his wounds, indeed he never fully recovered his health. Nobody knows who was behind the assassination attempt: a popular theory is that it was commissioned by the Soviet Union hierarchy who were deeply worried about the liberating effect that the popular Polish pope was having in his homeland and in other Communist countries. Or maybe it was an internal Vatican plot. His would-be assassin was eventually sentenced to life imprisonment but has never revealed who his paymasters—if any—were. Pope John Paul II visited him in prison in late December 1983. They conversed privately and afterward John Paul said, "What we talked about will have to remain a secret between him and me. I spoke to him as a brother whom I have pardoned and who has my complete trust."

On May 12, 1982, Pope John Paul II was the target of yet another assassination attempt. He was visiting Fatima in Portugal when a man rushed towards him in an attempt to stab him with a bayonet. Luckily security guards were able to grab the man before he could harm the Pope.

The failed attacker turned out to be an extremely conservative Spanish priest named Juan Maria Fernández y Krohn, who apparently opposed recent Catholic reforms. He served six years in prison.

Pope John Paul II had been a vigorous and healthy sportsman, and brought a renewed enthusiasm to the papacy. Until later life he had always been lucky with his health although the assassination attempts left him weaker. In the 1990s he had a number of cancer scares and in 1992 had a tumor removed from his colon. In 1993 he dislocated his shoulder and then broke his femur in 1994. In 1996 he had his appendix removed. Finally, in 2001 an orthopaedic surgeon confirmed widespread speculation that the pope was suffering form the onset of Parkinson's Disease, but the Vatican did not confirm this until 2003. By this time he was noticeably having difficulty with his speech and seemed to have trouble hearing clearly as well. In addition he was rarely seen to walk in public after a hip replacement led to severe arthritis in his right knee.

However, this physical disability never stopped Pope John Paul II from continuing his ministry and taking his message in person to the faithful with his lengthy international visits around the world. By all accounts despite his physical frailty his mind was as sharp as ever. But the weight of his office inevitably took a heavy toll on his constitution and although he publicly repudiated any thought of giving up the papacy, his personal private papers show that he was severely tempted in 2002, but as it was God's will that he was pope it was not for him to resign.

By September 2003 Pope John Paul II was obviously declining and renewed fears for his health surfaced when his right hand man Joseph Cardinal Ratzinger appealed for people to pray for the pope. This presaged a visit to the Gemelli Hospital in Rome on February 1, 2005 where John Paul was taken after a bout of influenza suffering from acute inflammation of the larynx and laryngo-spasm. On February 6 John Paul appeared at his hospital window to whisper the concluding lines of the Angelus blessing: he had clearly not recovered. As Easter arrived doubts were voiced about whether he would be able to participate in the service. For the first time in his papacy he missed the Ash Wednesday ceremonies but was able to return to the Vatican on Thursday February 10.

Two weeks later, on February 24, he was rushed back to the Gemelli Hospital were he underwent a tracheotomy to alleviate his breathing problems. From then on he was advised not to try to speak. He was however able to give a silent blessing from his hospital window on Sunday February 27 and Sunday March 6, and Cardinal Ratzinger insisted that the pope was still continuing his work and able to give clear instructions.

By Sunday March 13 John Paul had improved enough to speak to pilgrims during the *Angelus* and then to return home to the Vatican later that day. On March 20, Palm Sunday, John Paul appeared at his window over St Peter's Square and silently waved an olive branch to the thousands of pilgrims hoping for a glimpse of him. They cheered at the sight of him but he was only able to watch the Palm Sunday Mass on TV from his apartment.

Two days later the Vatican confirmed that John Paul IIs health had got worse and other church officials would take his place in the Vatican ceremonies. Then, on March 24, Cardinal Alfonso Lopez Trujillo having stood in for the pope said that John Paul was "serenely abandoning himself to God's will". The end was obviously in sight.

John Paul II appeared for the last time from his apartment window on March 27, Easter Sunday. He blessed the crowd while Angelo Cardinal Sodano read the *Urbi et Orbi* message. He clearly attempted to speak to his people but was sadly unable to utter a sound.

The exact chronicle of the last days of John Paul II are unclear. By March 31 he had a high fever caused by a urinary tract infection, but he did not return to hospital, probably because he wished to die at home in the Vatican. Later that same day the Vatican announced that he had received the Last Rites (properly called the Anointing of the Sick). John Paul II was clearly close to death. Early morning, April 1 the Vatican announced that Pope John Paul II had suffered a heart attack, this was quickly changed to a "cardiocirculatory collapse." Some media reports were already claiming that he was dead but this was denied by the Vatican who said that he had requested to be read the meditations said on the Stations of the Cross a few days earlier.

With the news that the Pope's life was drawing to a close thousands of the faithful felt drawn to St Peter's Square to pray for him and keep vigil outside his apartments. His last message was sent to those people, especially the young among them, "I came to you, now it's you who have come to me. I thank you."

Through that long evening and night anxious Catholics around the world waited for news: the Vatican conceded that the pope's kidneys had failed but that he remained conscious. On April 2 Father Jarek Cielecki reported that John Paul's last word were, "Amen."

Pope John Paul II died in his private apartments in the Vatican on April 3 aged 84, a few days after Easter, the holiest time of the year. His death certificate gave septic shock and heart failure as the prime causes of death. Waiting with him through his last hours were his two faithful Polish secretaries Archbishop Stanislaw Dziwisz and Mieczyslaw Mokrzycki, Marian Cardinal Jaworski, Archbishop Stanislaw Rylko and Father Tadeusz Styczeſ. Standing by were his three doctors and their nurses plus three nuns from the order of the Sacred Heart of Jesus.

When Pope John Paul II's death was reported to the thousands standing vigil in St Peter's Square the crowd clapped honoring the Italian custom as a sign of deep respect. Although devastated they followed the pope's command to celebrate his death as the passage to the next stage of his eternal life. Out of his 263 papal predecessors only two other popes throughout history have ruled for longer than John Paul II—this becomes three if St Peter himself is included.

People around the world mourned the passing of John Paul II but nowhere more so than in his native Poland. Six days of official mourning were declared and the state television cancelled all entertainment shows and broadcast mass instead. In addition people spontaneously gathered at the church in his hometown of Wadowice.

From around the world came messages of condolence and support, many flags flew at half mast as a sign of respect. John Paul had touched the hearts of millions through his work as supreme pontiff, in his efforts to bring peace to stricken lands and an end to world poverty, as well as through his personal examples of piety and suffering through the after effects of the assassination attempt and his long illness in his latter years. His staunch return to an old fashioned rigorous Catholicism had found favour with many Catholics.

John Paul II was not interested in reforming the Catholic Church to reflect modern times, instead he consistently gave speeches against abortion, homosexuality, and divorce, and in fact withdrew permission to publish from many eminent theologians who disagreed with him by broadcasting "unacceptable views" on subjects such as contraception and papal infallibility. He did however, extend the hand of friendship to other Christian branches of the worldwide Christian community as well as to Islam and Judaism. Many people credit him with hastening the collapse of Communism in Poland and then throughout the Eastern Bloc with his continuous promotion of non-violent revolution against such oppressive regimes.

In South America especially, a continent close to the papal heart, the mourning was extensive and public. In the United States all public buildings including the White House were ordered to fly flags at half mast until John Paul was buried. President George W Bush said that the world had lost a "champion of human freedom" who had been "an inspiration to millions of Americans." Across the world flags were lowered and official days of mourning declared.

During his pontificate Pope John Paul II created 482 saints and set in motion with beatification a further 1,338 people. This is more, even by the Vatican's estimation, than all of his predecessors combined who created 285 saints throughout history. Also, thanks to the sheer longevity of his pontificate, Pope John Paul II appointed 115 cardinals (it takes 118 to appoint the next pope), but given the fact that he outlived many of the cardinals he actually created 231 cardinals.

In addition John Paul II travelled extensively during his 26 year pontificate communicating with both the rich and poor of many lands. His early years of study really came to the fore as he was able to speak ten languages fluently, his native Polish of course, Italian for use in and around the Vatican, Russian, Slovak, Ukranian, German, French, Spanish, Portugese, and English, plus also Ecclesiastical Latin.

The body of John Paul II lay in state in St Peter's Basilica for three days while hundreds of thousands of people filed past to make their final respects. His body was on open display robed in crimson vestments, his head covered with a white bishop's mitre while his arm clasped his bishop's staff.

The funeral of Pope John Paul II was unique for the sheer number of dignatries and important leaders—both ecclesiastical and political—who attended. Millions of people around the watched the funeral mass live via satellite while an estimated two million crammed into Rome, many of them had journeyed all the way from Poland to attend the last ceremonies for their pope. An estimated 300,000 people crammed into St Peter's Square itself with further thousands thronging the surrounding streets as they watched the funeral mass on one of the 27 giant screens set up especially for the occasion. The crowd clapped and cheered with many chanting "Santo! Santo"!—a call for the pope to be canonized. In addition to the mourners some 15,000 security people were on duty to survey the crowds as the sheer numbers of people presented a security headache. At Kraków in Poland 800,000 people gathered together to listen to the funeral mass; many had stayed all night gathered around bonfires praying and celebrating the life and death of their beloved leader.

John Paul II was buried on Friday April 8, 2005 in a crypt under St Peter's Basilica. His cypress wood coffin was simply decorated with a cross and a large "M" for Mary. His body had been placed there during a private ceremony before 12 gentlemen ushers of the Vatican carried his coffin into St Peter's Square for the public ceremonies. His coffin was followed by 160 cardinals as it was placed on a bier on top of an elaborate Oriental carpet for the duration of the mass.

Cardinal Ratzinger delivered the homily in Italian on the life and works of Karel Wojtyla. "Today we bury his remains in the earth as a seed of immortality. Our hearts are full of sadness yet at the same time of joyful hope and profound gratitude. . . . We can be sure that our beloved pope is standing today at the window of the father's house, that he sees us and blesses us." Behind closed doors the homily was sealed in a lead tube and placed in the coffin along with all the medals coined during the pope's reign. His coffin was placed near the tomb believed to be that of St Peter, the first pope, on top of a mixture of bare earth from Poland and Vatican clay. His gravestone reads, "Johannes Paulus II 1920-2005." He now keeps company with 147 other popes.

The proceedings were watched by President Bush who attended as the first president in office to be present for a pope's funeral. Also there were former US presidents George Bush and Bill Clinton. In addition there were four kings, five queens, numerous lesser royals, at least 70 presidents and prime ministers and 14 important religious leaders.

Since the start of his Pontificate on October 16, 1978, Pope John Paul II has completed 104 pastoral visits outside of Italy and 146 within Italy . As Bishop of Rome he has visited 317 of the 333 parishes.

His principal documents include 14 encyclicals, 15 apostolic exhortations, 11 apostolic constitutions and 45 apostolic letters. The Pope has also published five books : "Crossing the Threshold of Hope" (October 1994); "Gift and Mystery: On the 50th Anniversary of My Priestly Ordination" (November 1996); "Roman Triptych - Meditations", a book of poems (March 2003); "Rise, Let Us Be On Our Way" (May 2004) and "Memory and Identity" (pubblication spring 2005).

John Paul II has presided at 147 beatification ceremonies ( 1,338 Blesseds proclaimed ) and 51 canonization ceremonies ( 482 Saints ) during his pontificate. He has held 9 consistories in which he created 231 (+ 1 in pectore) cardinals. He has also convened six plenary meetings of the College of Cardinals.

From 1978 to today the Holy Father has presided at 15 Synods of Bishops : six ordinary (1980, 1983, 1987, 1990, 1994, 2001), one extraordinary (1985) and eight special (1980, 1991, 1994, 1995, 1997, 1998[2] and 1999).

No other Pope has encountered so many individuals like John Paul II: to date, more than 17,600,000 pilgrims have participated in the General Audiences held on Wednesdays (more than 1,160). Such figure is without counting all other special audiences and religious ceremonies held [more than 8 million pilgrims during the Great Jubilee of the Year 2000 alone] and the millions of faithful met during pastoral visits made in Italy and throughout the world. It must also be remembered the numerous government personalities encountered during 38 official visits and in the 738 audiences and meetings held with Heads of State, and even the 246 audiences and meetings with Prime Ministers.

| | | KAROL JÓSEF WOJTYLA |
|---|---|---|
| 1920 | May 18 | Born in Wadowice (Kraków), Poland. |
| | June 20 | Baptized by the military chaplain P. Franciszek Zak. |
| | | Lived with his parents at Rynek 2, (now Via Koscielna 7, apt. no. 4). |
| 1926 | September 15 | Attended the elementary school, and then the prep years of secondary school "Marcin Wadowita". |
| 1929 | April 13 | His mother dies. |
| 1930 | June | Admitted to the State Secondary School for boys, "Marcin Wadowita". |
| 1932 | December 5 | His brother Edmund dies. |
| 1933 | June 14 | Finishes the third form of Secondary School. |
| 1934-1938 | | His first student theatrical performances in Wadowice; during Secondary School he is president of the Society of Mary. |
| 1935 | September | Participates in military training exercises at Hermanice. |
| | December 14 | Admitted into the Society of Mary. |
| 1938 | May | Receives the Sacrament of Confirmation. |
| | May 14 | Completes leaving exams at Secondary School. |
| | June 22 | Enrolls in the Faculty of Philosophy (course of Polish Philosophy) at Jagellonian University, Kraków. |
| 1939 | February 6 | Joins the Student Society at the Jagellonian University (Eucharistic and charity section). |
| | July | University military training camp at Ozomla, near Sadowa Wiszna for Polish and Ukraine students. |
| | November 2 | Registers for the second year university courses in Literature and Philosophy. |
| 1940 | February | Meets Jan Tyranowski, a man of profound spirituality. Introduces Wojtyla to the writings of John of the Cross and Teresa d'Avila. |
| | | Participates in the underground theater directed by Tadeusz Kudlilski. |
| | November 1 | He earns a living and forestalls deportation and imprisonment, as a stone cutter in a quarry at Zakrzówek, Kraków. |
| 1941 | February 18 | His father dies. |
| | August | Receives into his house the family of Mieczyslaw Kotlarczyk, founder of the live words theater (Rhapsody). |
| | November 1 | First presentation of Król Duch (The Spirit King) by Jiliusz Slowacki. |
| 1942 | Spring | Transferred to Solvay chemical plant. |
| | October | Begins clandestine studies for the priesthood in Kraków's underground seminary; registers in the Faculty of Theology of the Jagellonian University. |
| 1943 | March | Takes the lead role of "Samuel Zborowski" by Juliusz Slowacki making his first appearance on the theatrical scene. |
| 1943-1944 | | Second year of theology studies. Continues to work in the Solvay chemical plant. |
| 1944 | Feb 29 - Mar 12 | Hit by an automobile; recovery in hospital. |
| | August | Archbishop Adam Stefan Sapieha transfers him, to the Archbishop's Residence where he remains until the end of the war. |
| | November 9 | Receives the tonsure. |
| | December 17 | Receives the first two minor orders. |
| 1944-1945 | | Third year of theological studies. |
| | April 9 | Elected vice-president of the student organization "Bratnia Pomoc" (Fraternal Help) at Jagellonian University. Serves in this capacity until the end of May 1946. |
| 1945-1946 | | Fourth year of theological studies. |
| | December 12 | Receives the two other minor orders. |
| 1946 | October 13 | Sub-diaconate. |
| | October 20 | Diaconate. |
| | November 1 | Ordained a priest. As on the preceding occasions, he received Holy Orders from the hands of Archbishop Metropolitan Adam Sapieha in his private chapel. |
| | November 2 | Celebrates his first Mass in the crypt of St. Leonard at Wavel. |
| | November 15 | Leaves Poland to begin studies in Rome. |
| | November 26 | Registers at the Angelicum University. |
| 1947 | July 3 | Earns a licentiate in theology. |
| | Summer | With Fr. Starowieyski he travels to France, Belgium and Holland. In the area of Charleroi he carries out his pastoral activities with the Polish workers. |
| 1948 | June 14-19 | Defends his thesis "The Problems of Faith in the Works of St. John of the Cross"; earns a doctorate in philosophy. |
| | July | Returns from Rome to Poland. |
| | July 8 | Sent as assistant pastor to Niegowil near Gdów. |
| | December 16 | Earns a master's degree in theology at the Jagellonian University in Kraków (1942-1946). Earns a doctorate in sacred theology in the Faculty of Theology. |
| 1949 | August | Recalled to Kraków to be assistant pastor at St. Florian's. |
| 1951 | September 1 | Archbishop Baziak puts him on leave (until 1953) to complete his qualifying exams for a university position. |
| 1953 | October | Gives a course in Catholic social ethics for the students of fourth year theology at the Jagellonian University. |
| | December 1-3 | Completes his qualifying exams by presenting his thesis on the "ethical system of Max Scheler". |
| 1956 | December 1 | Appointed to the Chair of Ethics at the Catholic University of Lublin. |
| 1957 | November 15 | The Central Qualifying Committee approves his appointment as free docent. |
| 1958 | July 4 | Appointed Auxiliary Bishop to Archbishop Mons. Eugeniusz Baziak of Kraków. |
| | September 28 | Ordained Bishop in the Cathedral of Wavel. |
| 1960 | During 1960 | First edition of "Love and Responsibility" (ed. by TNKUL). |

| 1962 | April 15 | Member of the Polish Episcopal Commission for Education. |
|---|---|---|
| | July 16 | After the death of Archbishop Baziak, named Vicar Capitular. |
| | October 5 | Leaves for Rome to participate in the first session of the Second Vatican Council (October 11 - December 8). |
| 1963 | Oct 6 - Dec 4 | Participates in the II Session of the Second Vatican Council. |
| | December 5-15 | Pilgrimage to the Holy Land with various Bishops of different nationalities present at the Council. |
| | December 30 | Designated Metropolitan Bishop of Kraków. |
| 1964 | January 13 | Papal Bull for the appointment of Archbishop of Kraków. |
| | March 8 | Installation ceremony. |
| | September 10 | Leaves for the III session of the Second Vatican Council (September 14 - November 21); at its conclusion makes a pilgrimage to the Holy Land. |
| 1965 | Jan 31 - Apr 6 | Participates in the work on Schema XIII, Gaudium et spes on the Church in the contemporary world. |
| | Sep 14 - Dec 8 | IV Session and solemn closing of the Second Vatican Council. |
| | November 18 | Letter of Reconciliation of the Polish Bishops to the German Bishops, containing the famous words "We forgive and ask forgiveness". |
| 1966 | December 29 | Episcopal Commission for the Apostolate of the Laity is established; Archbishop Wojtyla is made President. |
| | During 1966 | Present at the numerous celebrations of the Millennium of the Baptism of Poland. |
| 1967 | April 13-20 | Participates in the first meeting of the Council for the Laity. |
| | May 29 | Paul VI announces the next Consistory. Among the names of the new Cardinals elect is that of Karol Wojtyla. |
| | June 21 | Leaves for the Consistory. |
| | June 28 | Consecrated Cardinal in the Sistine Chapel, by Pope Paul VI - titular S. Cesareo in Palatio. |
| | October 29 | Reception ceremony of the Black Madonna of Czlstochowa for the purpose of visitation within the Archdiocese of Kraków. |
| 1968 | February 18 | Takes possession of the titular Church, S. Cesareo in Palatio, Rome. |
| | September 25 | "Ad limina" visit to Rome. |
| | December 15 | Visitation of the Black Madonna concludes in the Archdiocese of Kraków. Cardinal Wojtyla attends ceremonies in 120 parishes throughout the archdiocese. |
| 1969 | January 10 | Official address becomes the Archbishop's Residence in Via Franciszkanska 3. |
| | February 28 | During his visitation to the parish of Corpus Domini he makes a visit to the Jewish Community and to the Synagogue in the Kazimierz section of Kraków. |
| | March 15 | Approval of the statutes of the Episcopal Conference; Cardinal Wojtyla is Vice-President of the Conference. |
| | October 11-28 | With his return from America he participates in the First Extraordinary Synod of Bishops as a Pontifical nominated Member. |
| 1970 | May 29 | Participates with other Polish priests in St. Peters at the celebrations for the 50th anniversary of the priesthood of Paul VI. |
| | May 30 | Participates in the mass of Paolo VI. Audience in occasion of the celebrations for the 50th anniversary of the priesthood of Paul VI. |
| 1971 | Janurary 8 | Convokes the Preparatory Commission of the Archdiocesan Synod of Kraków. |
| | September 27 | Leaves for the II General Assembly of the Synod of Bishops (September 30 - November 6). |
| | October 5 | Is elected to the Council of the Secretary General of the Synod of Bishops. |
| | October 17 | Participates at the beatification of Fr. Maximilian Kolbe. |
| 1972 | During 1972 | Publishes Foundations of Renewal: A Study on the Implementation of the Second Vatican Council. |
| 1973 | March 2-9 | Participates in the Eucharistic Congress in Australia. Stops at Manila (Philippines) and New Guinea. |
| | June 30 | First meeting of the commission of experts on the Provincial Synod presided over by Cardinal Wojtyla. |
| | Sep 26 - Oct 5 | "Ad limina" visit to Rome. |
| | October 5 | Audience with Paul VI. |
| 1974 | April 17-25 | In Italy, participates in meetings commemorating the VII Centenary of St. Thomas where he gives a paper (April 23). |
| | June 28 | In Rome, participates in the celebrations for the anniversary of the coronation of Paul VI and for the consecration of Bishop Andrzej Maria Deskur. |
| | November 1-3 | Visit to San Giovanni Rotondo. (He was there for the first time during his student years and met with Padre Pio). |
| 1975 | February 8-9 | First National Assembly of Physicians and Theologians, convoked by Cardinal Wojtyla at Kraków. |
| 1976 | March 7-13 | Gives the spiritual exercises at the Vatican, in the presence of Pope Paul VI, the meditations from which have been published as A Sign of Contradiction. |
| 1977 | June 23 | Receives a doctorate "honoris causa" from Johannes Guttenberg University, Mainz. |
| 1978 | August 11-12 | Present at the funeral of Paul VI. |
| | August 25 | Conclave begins. |
| | August 26 | John Paul I (Albino Luciani) is elected Pope. |
| | August 30 | John Paul I receives Cardinals and Card. Wojtyla in private audience. |
| | 3 September | He is present at the inauguration ceremony of the pontificate of John Paul I. |
| | October 3-4 | Leaves for the funeral of Pope John Paul I. |
| | October 14 | Conclave begins. |
| | October 16 | Cardinal Karol Wojtyla is elected 264th Pope at approximately 5:15 p.m. He is the 263rd Successor of Peter. |

**Above:** *An undated file photo shows Karol Josef Wojtyla, together with his mother Emilia Kaczorowska. The Pope was born on May 18, 1920 in Krakow, Poland.*

**Left:** *Karol Wojtyla, later known as Pope John Paul II, poses with a candle after receiving his First Communion in Wadowice, in his home archidiocese of Krakow, Poland in this undated file photo.*

*Right:* A 1930 file photo shows ten-year old Karol Wojtyla, later known as Pope John Paul II (2nd row 2ndR) with classmates in Wadovice, Poland.

*Below:* An undated file photo shows ten-year old altar boy Karol Wojtyla, later known as Pope John Paul II in Wadovice, Poland.

*An undated file photo shows Karol Wojtyla, later known as Pope John Paul II in Wadovice, Poland.*

***Right:*** *Undated file photo of Pope John Paul II as the young priest Father Karol Wojtyla, when he was in the seminary in Poland.*

*A 1955 file photo shows Karol Wojtyla, later known as Pope John Paul II in*
*a boat on the river Drawa, Poland.*

*A 1959 file photo shows Karol Wojtyla, later known as Pope John Paul II as archbishop.*

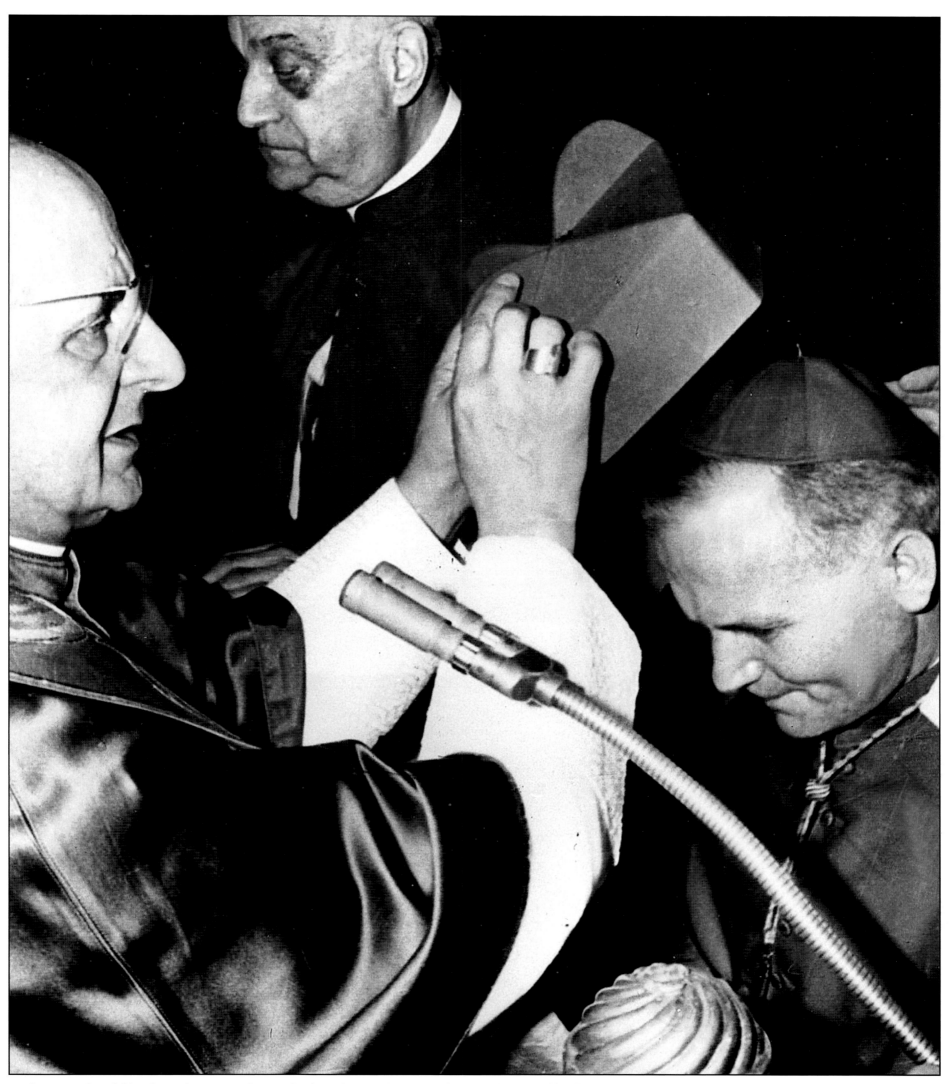

*Left: An undated file photo shows Karol Wojtyla, later known as Pope John Paul II as archbishop in Krakau, Poland.*

*Above: A file photo shows Pope Paul VI nominating archbishop Karol Wojtyla, later known as Pope John Paul II, as cardinal on June 26, 1967.*

## In The Beginning: John Paul II's First Homily

1. "You are the Christ, the Son of the living God" (Mt. 16:16)
Simon son of Jona pronounced these words in the territory of Caesarea Philippi. It is true that he expressed them with his own language, with a deep, lively and heartfelt conviction; but those words do not have their fountain, their source, in him: "because neither flesh or blood have revealed it to you, but my Father who is in heaven" (Mt. 16:17). These were words of Faith.
They mark the beginning of the mission of Peter in the history of salvation, in the history of the People of God. From that moment, from such a confession of Faith, the sacred history of the salvation of the People of God was to acquire a new dimension: to express itself in the historic dimension of the Church. This church-dimension of the history of the People of God has its beginnings, its birth, precisely in these words of Faith. This church-dimension of the history of the People of God is tied to the man who pronounced these words of Faith: "You are Peter-rock-and upon you, as upon a rock, I shall build my Church."

2. This very day and in this place, the same words need to be again pronounced and listened to: "You are the Christ, the Son of the living God."
Yes, Brother and Sisters, Sons and Daughters, those words above all!
What they contain opens to our eyes the mystery of the living God, the mystery that the Son knows and has brought close to us. No one, in fact, has brought the living God close to men, no one has revealed Him as He himself alone has done. In our knowledge of God, in our journey towards God we are totally bound to the power of these words: "Whoever sees me, sees indeed the Father." He who is Infinite, inscrutable, ineffable has brought himself close to us in Jesus Christ, the only-begotten Son, born of the Virgin Mary in the stable of Bethlehem.
–All of you who already have the immense fortune to believe,
–all of you who are still searching for God,
–and even you who are tormented by doubt:
come and welcome one more time-today in this sacred place-the words pronounced by Simon Peter. In those words is the faith of the Church. In those same words is the new truth-in fact the last and definitive truth about man: the Son of the living God. "You are the Christ, the Son of the living God!"

3. Today the new Bishop of Rome solemnly begins his ministry and the mission of Peter. In this City, in fact, Peter unfolded and fulfilled the mission the Lord entrusted to him.
The Lord confronted him and said: "when you were younger you girded yourself and you went where you chose; but when you are old you will hold out your hands, and someone else will gird you and take you where you do not wish" (Jn. 21:18).
Peter came to Rome!
What guided and led him to this City, heart of the Roman Empire, if not obedience to the inspiration that came from the Lord? Perhaps this fisherman of Galilee would not have wanted to come all the way here. Perhaps he would have preferred to stay there, on the banks of the lake of Gennesaret, with his boat, with his nets. However, guided by the Lord, obedient to his inspiration, he came here!
According to an ancient tradition (which has also found magnificent literary expression in a novel by Henryk Sienkiewicz), during the persecution by Nero, Peter wanted to abandon Rome. However, the Lord intervened: he went to meet Peter. Peter turned to him and asked: "Quo vadis, Domine?" (Where are you going, Lord?). The Lord immediately answered him: "I go to Rome to be crucified for the second time." Peter turned back to Rome and he stayed here until his own crucifixion.
Yes, Brothers and Sisters, Sons and Daughters, Rome is the See of Peter. Through the centuries new Bishops have always succeeded Peter in this See. Today a new Bishop ascends to the Roman Chair of Peter, a Bishop full of anxiety, knowing his unworthiness. How could anyone not be anxious when facing the greatness of such a calling, and when facing the universal mission of this Roman See?!
Today in Rome a Bishop who is not a Roman ascends to the See of Peter. A Bishop who is a son of Poland. However, from this moment on, even he becomes a Roman. Yes, a Roman! Furthermore, he is a son of a nation whose history, from its first awakenings, and whose thousand-year traditions are marked by a lively, strong, never-interrupted, heartfelt and living link with the See of Peter, a nation that has always remained faithful to the See of Rome. How inscrutable the plan of divine Providence!

4. In past centuries, when the Successor of Peter took possession of his See, the triple crown, the tiara, was placed on his head. The last man so crowned was Pope Paul VI in 1963. However, after the solemn rite of coronation he never again used the triple crown, and left to his Successors the freedom to decide about it.
Pope John Paul the First, whose memory is so alive in our hearts, did not wish the triple crown, and today his Successor does not want it. It is not the time, in fact, to return to a rite that, perhaps unjustly, was considered a symbol of the temporal power of the Popes. Our time invites us, pushes us, obligates us to look to the Lord, and to plunge into a humble and devout meditation on the mystery of the supreme power of Christ himself.

He who was born of the Virgin Mary, the so-called son of the carpenter, the Son of the living God, as Peter confessed, came to make all of us "a kingdom of priests."
The Second Vatican Council has reminded us of the mystery of this power, and of the fact that the mission of Christ-Priest, Teaching Prophet, King-continues in the Church. Everyone, the whole people of God has a part in this threefold mission. Perhaps in the past, we put the triple crown on the head of the Pope to express by such a symbol that the whole hierarchical order of the Church of Christ, all of Christ's "sacred power" exercised in the Church, is nothing else but service, service that has one goal alone: that the whole People of God take part in this threefold mission of Christ, and remain always under the Lord's power. His power comes not from the powers of this world, but from the heavenly Father and from the mystery of the Cross and of the Resurrection.
The absolute power of the Lord is even sweet and gentle. So, it answers all the depths of man; it answers his highest aspirations of intellect, of will, of heart. His power does not speak with a language of force, but it expresses itself in charity and in truth.
The new Successor of Peter in the See of Rome raises up today a fervent, humble, trusting prayer: "O Christ! Make me able to become and to be a servant of your unique power! A servant of your gentle power! A servant of your power that has no sundown! Make me able to be a servant! In fact, a servant of your servants!"

5. Brothers and Sisters! Do not be afraid to welcome Christ, and to accept his power!
Help the Pope and all who want to serve Christ and, with the power of Christ, to serve the human person and all of humanity!
Do not be afraid! Open, in fact, break down the doors for Christ!
To his saving power, open the borders of the Nations, the economic systems, the political systems, the vast fields of culture, of civilization, of development. Do not be afraid! Christ knows "what is in the heart of man." He alone knows it!
So often today, man does not know what he carries inside himself, in the depth of his soul, of his heart. So often he is uncertain of the meaning of his life on earth. He is invaded by doubt that shifts into desperation. So then, allow-I beg you, I implore with humility and confidence-allow Christ to speak to man. Christ alone has words of life, yes, of eternal life.
Exactly today the entire Church celebrates "World Mission Sunday." The Church prays, meditates and acts so that Christ's words of life may reach all men and be received by them as a message of hope, of salvation, of total freedom.

6. I thank all those here who have chosen to take part in this solemn inauguration of the ministry of the new Successor of Peter.
I heartily thank the Heads of States, the Representatives of Authorities and the Government Delegations for their presence that so honors me.
Thank you, Most Eminent Cardinals of the Holy Roman Church!
I thank you, beloved Brother Bishops.
Thank you, Priests!
To you Sisters and Brothers, members of the Religious Orders and Congregations! Thank!
Thank you, Romans!
Thank you to the pilgrims gathered from all the world!
Thank you to all who are joined to this Sacred Rite through the Radio and the Television!

7. [The Holy Father begins to speak in Polish, and then briefly explains, as follows, what he said in Polish.]
This was an appeal and an invitation to prayer for the new Pope, an appeal expressed in the Polish language. Making the same appeal I turn to all the sons and daughters of the Catholic Church. Remember me today and always in your prayer.
[The Holy Father begins to speak in French. Afterwards, he says the following in English.]
To all of you who speak English I offer in the name of Christ a cordial greeting. I count on the support of your prayers and your good will in carrying out my mission of service to the Church and mankind. May Christ give you his grace and his peace, overturning the barriers of division and making all things one in him.
[Then, the Holy Father speaks in several other languages before concluding as follows.]
I open my heart to all the Brothers and Sisters of the Churches and Christian Communities, greeting, in particular, you who are present here, even as I look forward to our next personal meeting; but for now I express to you sincere appreciation for your choosing to attend this solemn rite.

Once again, I turn to all men, to each man (and with what veneration the apostle of Christ must pronounce this word: man!).

Pray for me!

Help me so that I can serve you! Amen.

**Above:** *White smoke rising from the Sistine Chapel, traditionally the result of the last ballots being burnt and the first sign that a new Pope has been elected.*

**Left:** *Workers seal the entrances of the Sistine Chapel before the start of the election of a new Pope in Rome.*

**Below:** *111 Cardinals pray inside the Sistine Chapel before the start of the election of a new Pope in Rome in this August 25, 1978 file photo. The College of Cardinals, made up of the Church's highest-ranking prelates, has been empowered to elect Popes since the twelfth century.*

**Overleaf:** *Pope John Paul II seen in 1978 in Rome after visiting Polish Bishop Andrej Maria Deskur at the Gemelli Hospital, a few days after his election as pope.*

*Pope John Paul II wearing a traditional highlanders gown and hat raises his hands just after arriving at the Balice airport in Krakow during his first visit to his native country in June 1979.*

*Pope John Paul II lies seriously wounded in his open car moments after he was shot by Turkish Mehmet Ali Agca in St Peter's Square in this May 13, 1981.*

*__Below:__ Pope John Paul II meets with his would-be assasin, Turkish gunman Mehmet Ali Agca in his prison cell in December 1983. Italy granted Agca clemency June 13, the presidential palace said. Agca has still to serve part of a sentence in Turkey for killing a journalist in 1978.*

**Through Faith Man Accepts in a Free and Convincing Manner the Truths Contained in God's Revelation**

John Paul II, General Audience, April 17, 1985

*Left: Pope John Paul II greets an unidentified official of Italy's 'American Circus' while acrobat Giuly Cristiani of Italy leaves after kissing the hand of the pontiff, at the end of their performance in the Vatican, January 23, 1985. Acrobats and other circus artists performed for the pontiff for about an hour in the Paul VI Auditorium during his weekly general audience.*

*Right: Pope John Paul II imparts Urbi et Orbi blessing to the City and the World in St. Peter's Square, Vatican City, April 17, 1985, after the celebration of the Easter ceremony. About 250,000 pilgrims gathered in the square in Rome.*

The originality of faith consists in the essentially supernatural character of knowledge which it derives from God's grace and from the gifts of the Holy Spirit. It must likewise be said that faith possesses its own authentically human originality. We find in it all the characteristics of rational and reasonable conviction in regard to the truth contained in divine revelation. Such conviction, or certainty, corresponds perfectly to the dignity of the person as a rational and free being.

Among the documents of the Second Vatican Council, the Declaration on Religious Liberty throws light on this problem. It begins with the words Dignitatis Humanae, and we read there among other things:

"It is one of the major tenets of Catholic doctrine that man's response to God in faith must be free: no one therefore is to be forced to embrace the Christian faith against his own will. This doctrine is contained in the word of God and it was constantly proclaimed by the Fathers of the Church. The act of faith is of its very nature a free act. Man, redeemed by Christ the Savior and through Christ Jesus called to be God's adopted son, cannot give his adherence to God revealing himself unless, under the drawing of the Father, he offers to God the reasonable and free submission of faith. It is therefore completely in accord with the nature of faith that in matters religious every manner of coercion on the part of men should be excluded" (DH 10).

"God calls men to serve him in spirit and in truth, hence they are bound in conscience but they stand under no compulsion. God has regard for the dignity of the human person whom he himself created and man is to be guided by his own judgment and he is to enjoy freedom. This truth appears at its height in Christ Jesus" (DH 11).

*1. Christ bore witness to the truth*

Here the conciliar document indicates in what way Christ sought to "stir up and strengthen the faith in the hearers" by excluding all coercion. He bore definitive witness to the truth of his Gospel through the cross and the resurrection, "He refused to impose the truth by force on those who spoke against it.... His rule...is established by witnessing to the truth and by hearing the truth, and it extends its dominion by the love whereby Christ, lifted up on the cross, draws all men to himself" (DH 11). Christ then handed on to the apostles the same method of convincing in regard to the truth of the Gospel.

Precisely because of this freedom, faith - which we express by the word "credo" - possesses its own human authenticity and originality, besides the divine. It expresses conviction and certainty about the truth of revelation, by virtue of an act of free will. This structural voluntariness of faith in no way implies that faith is optional and that an attitude of fundamental indifference would be justified. It only means that man is called to respond

with the free adherence of his entire being to the invitation and gift of God. The same conciliar document which deals with the problem of religious liberty underlines clearly that faith is a matter of conscience.

"It is in accordance with their dignity as persons - that is, beings endowed with reason and free will and therefore privileged to bear personal responsibility - that all men should be at once impelled by nature and also bound by a moral obligation to seek the truth, especially religious truth. They are also bound to adhere to the truth, once it is known, and to order their whole lives in accord with the demands of truth" (DH 2). If this is the essential argument in favor of the right to religious liberty, it is also the fundamental motive for the fact that this same liberty must be correctly understood and observed in social life.

As regards personal decisions, "everybody has the duty and therefore the right to seek the truth in religious matters in order that, through the use of suitable means, he may prudently form judgments of conscience which are sincere and true.
"Truth, however, is to be sought after in a manner proper to the dignity of the human person and his social nature. The inquiry is to be free, carried on with the aid of teaching or instruction, communication and dialogue, in the course of which men explain to one another the truth they have discovered, or think they have discovered, in order thus to assist one another in the quest for truth. Moreover, as the truth is discovered, it is by a personal assent that men are to adhere to it" (DH 3).

In these words we find a very striking characteristic of our "credo" as a profoundly human act corresponding to the dignity of man as a person. This correspondence is expressed in the relationship with the truth by means of the interior freedom and the responsibility of conscience of the believing subject.

This doctrine, drawn from the conciliar declaration on religious liberty (Dignitatis Humanae), also serves to show the importance of a systematic catechesis, for two reasons. First, it makes possible the knowledge of the truth of God's plan of love which is contained in divine revelation. Secondly, it helps to adhere ever more firmly to the truth already known and accepted by faith.

**Left:** *Pope John Paul II blesses the crowd before his departure from the Belgian town of Ieper after a brief visit May 17, 1985. The Pope is on a five day tour of Belgium.*

**Below:** *Pope John Paul II in a gondola in the grand canal of the Venice lagoon during the Pontiff's visit to Venice June 16, 1985.*

*Pope John Paul II greets the crowds in Kinshasa, Zaire August 15, 1985 with Cardinal Malula.*

*Pope John Paul II wears a protective miners hat inside an elevator on his way to visit a mine shaft 370m underground in the Monteponi mines in Iglesias, Sardinia, October 18, 1985.*

*Pope John Paul II waters a freshly planted Mango tree on the lawn next to the Mahatma Gandhi Memorial in New Delhi February 1, 1986. Assisting him is New Delhi's Director of horticulture Dev Matt, who promised to send the first Mango to the Pope.*

*Pope John Paul II blesses dancers as he arrives for a mass at the Indira Gandhi Stadium in New Delhi, February 2, 1986.*

*Pope John Paul II holds hands with Mother Teresa after visiting the Casa del Cuore Puro, Mother Teresa's home for the destitute and dying in the eastern Indian city of Calcutta, February 3, 1986.*

*Above:* Pope John Paul II blesses the crowd as he is escorted by a Fijian warrior prior to a mass at Albert Park in Suva, Fiji, November 21, 1986.

*Right:* Pope John Paul II is helped on with a Maori cloak during traditional Maori welcoming ceremonies upon arrival in Auckland, New Zealand, November 22, 1986. The cloak is made from native bird feathers.

## ADDRESS OF JOHN PAUL II

## TO THE WORKERS IN THE FACTORY "TRANSFIELD LIMITED"

Sydney (Australia), 26 November 1986

Dear Friends,

1. I thank you for the way you have endorsed the kind words of welcome addressed to me, and I trust you can see that I am very happy to be here with you. You may know that I, too, was a worker for some years in a quarry and in a factory. These were important and useful years in my life. I am grateful for having had that opportunity to reflect deeply on the meaning and dignity of human work in its relationship to the individual, the family, the nation, and the whole social order. Those years allowed one to share in a specific way in God's creative activity and to experience work in the light of the Cross and Resurrection of Christ.

One of my reasons for coming here is to tell you, and all the workers of Australia, how much I admire faithfulness and dedication to ordinary work. Australia is a great country because working people like yourselves go about their tasks day after day with both cheerfulness and seriousness, earning their bread by the sweat of their brow, producing goods and services for their fellow citizens, and thus gradually bringing to perfection a world that was created by a good and loving God.

2. No doubt many of you have reflected from time to time that Jesus Christ himself, although the Son of God, chose to be an ordinary worker for most of his earthly life, toiling away as a carpenter in Nazareth. There is no shortage of lessons to be learned from the life of Jesus the Worker. It is only right, then, that his Church should bring his message into the working world and to workers. In the past, the Church has consistently opposed ways of thinking which would reduce workers to mere "things" that could be relegated to unemployment and redundancy if the economics of industrial development seemed to demand it. The students among you can consult the writings of my predecessors – going back to Leo XIII almost a hundred years ago – who treated at length topics such as the rights of workers, ownership, property, working hours, just wages and workers' associations.

Perhaps you have heard that five years ago I, too, wrote an Encyclical Letter on Human Work. My aim was to cast new light on the whole area of human work, an important subject where there are always fresh hopes but also fresh fears and dangers.

3. Among the many new elements that affect human work I wish to mention today the rapid development of technology. There is an aspect of this we can admire: in technology we can see ourselves as more than ever "subduing the earth" and gaining dominion over it. Technology itself is the work of human hands and human minds, and it enables us to produce other beautiful and useful things. This is admirable if the human person is clearly the master. But in large factories or on extended worksites, the number, size and complexity of the machines used can make the worker seem merely a part of the machine, just another cog in the whole process of production.

Many machines these days require operators with specialized training. But after being trained for a highly skilled job, the worker may suddenly discover that a new invention has made his machine obsolete and uneconomical. He may be too old to be trained a second time, or perhaps the firm employing him may go out of business. The result is that whole industries can be dislocated7 and individuals and families reduced to poverty, suffering and despair.

Despite the complexity of the problem we cannot give up. All the resources of human inventiveness and good will must be brought to bear, in order to help solve the social problems of our day connected with work. It is important to have clear ideas of the principles and priorities to be followed. In this context I wish to proclaim again my own profound conviction " that human work is a key, probably the essential key, to the whole social question, if we try to see the question really from the point of view of man's good".

4. People need to work, not just to earn money for the necessities of life, but also to fulfil their calling to share in the creative activity of God. The human satisfaction that comes from work well done shows how profoundly the Creator has inscribed the law of work in the heart of man.

The goods of the world belong to the whole human family. Normally a person will need to work in order to have a necessary share of these good things. In the early Christian community, Saint Paul insisted that willingness to work was a condition for being able to eat: "If a man will not work, let him not eat". In special situations, society can and must assist those who are in need and cannot work. Yet even in these special circumstances, people still have a desire for personal fulfilment, and this can be achieved only through some form or other of worthwhile human activity.

Thus those who are forced to retire early, as well as those who are still young and strong but cannot find work, may experience profound discouragement and feel that they are useless. These feelings may lead some to seek consolation in alcohol, drugs and other forms of behaviour harmful to themselves and to society.

We all need to feel that we are truly productive and useful members of our community. It is our right. And since the pace of technological change is likely to increase, it is vital for us to face all the serious problems that affect the well-being of workers.

5. No one has a simple and easy solution to all the problems connected with human work. But I offer for your consideration two basic principles. First, it is always the human person who is the purpose of work. It must be said over and over again that work is for man, not man for work. Man is indeed "the true purpose of the whole process of production". Every consideration of the value of work must begin with man, and every solution proposed to the problems of the social order must recognize the primacy of the human person over things. Secondly, the task of finding solution cannot be entrusted to any single group in society: people cannot look solely to governments as if they alone can End solutions; nor to big business, nor to small enterprises, nor to union officials, nor to individuals in the work force. All individuals and all groups must be concerned with both the problems and their solutions.

6. The Church is profoundly convinced that "the rights of the human person are the key element in the whole of the social moral order". She has long recognized the right of workers to form associations. The purpose of such associations is to promote social justice by defending the vital interests of workers and by contributing to the common good. It is important for the members to play an active and responsible role in these associations. Hence you must make sure that the leaders of your workers' associations really have at heart all the material and human needs of the members. They must also remember that the solution to any dispute must be fair to all sides, must serve the common good of society, and must take into account the economic and social situation of the country. Only if the economy as a whole is healthy will it be possible to make sufficient work available for workers, especially the young.

7. People are realizing more and more clearly that what happens in one part of the world has effects elsewhere. Worldwide problems demand worldwide solutions through the solidarity of all. No country can isolate itself from the common challenge. Union leaders and leaders of employer associations, as well as government agencies, need to work together in order to face the wide range of challenges. Every partner in this common endeavour should act on the conviction that everyone has a basic right to work in order to have a fair share of the world's goods. It must also be stressed that all the partners have a duty to work for solutions that respect the dignity of the individual and the common good of society. Economic problems cannot be separated from the ethical and social aspects of life in society.

8. On the national and local level industrial relations also require a spirit of understanding and cooperation rather than one of opposition and conflict. In all disputes, a just and peaceful solution will be possible only if all parties are, and remain, ready to talk. Always keep open the lines of communication, and remember that if disputes are not solved quickly, it is above all the weak and need who suffer.

Fortunately for Australia, your most cherished traditions place great value on equality and mutual support, especially in difficult times. The word "mate" has rich and positive connotations in your language. I pray that this tradition of solidarity will always flourish among you and will never be looked upon as old-fashioned.

Australia also has a long and proud tradition of settling industri,21 disputes and promoting cooperation by its almost unique system of arbitration and conciliation. Over the years this system has helped to defend the right of workers and promote their well-being, while at the same time taking into account the needs and the future of the whole community.

9. I make a special appeal to you workers to be always honest in your collaboration with others. I appeal to you to be especially conscious of all those in need, to give them practical help and to offer them your solidarity. I have been told that you have an organization for promoting development in poorer countries. For this I congratulate you, and I thank you. But you must be active too in helping the needy in your own midst, who include the unemployed, many young people, Aboriginal people, the sick, the disabled, the refugees and the new settlers.

10. I began by making reference to the new question and problems, fears and dangers that surround us because of the development and rapid use of the new technology. This technology is part of the accumulated wealth of the human family and a part of it belongs to you too. It is to be judged by the help it gives you in your work and lives. Always remember that the worker is always more important than both profits and machines. Dear friends, workers of Australia: it is up to you to make use of the new technology and press on with the task of building a society of justice and fraternal love – a society that extends well beyond the boundaries of Australia. It is God himself who strengthens your arms, enlightens your minds and purifies your hearts for this great work.

*Pope John Paul II, wearing an industrial hard hat meets workers at a Sydney steel-fabricating works in Sydney November 26 1986 during the third day of his Australian visit.*

*Olga Polak, age 3, presents Pope John Paul II flowers November 27, 1986 after she rushed from the crowd upon his arrival at Melbourne airport.*

Those of you who believe in Jesus Christ and accept his Gospel as the blueprint of your lives know that work has an even deeper meaning when it is seen in its relationship to the Lord's Cross and Resurrection. United with Christ in baptism, you are called to share through your work in Christ's mission of salvation and service to humanity. When offered to God in union with the work of Christ, your own work takes on an even greater value and higher dignity. Jesus Christ, the Son of God, who during his earthly life belonged so fully to the "working world", looks for ever with love on human work.

And for all of you in this vast land, whatever may be your religious convictions or the nature of your work, I pray that you may experience the uplifting and exhilarating awareness of working with the Creator in perfecting his design and plan for the world. All of this is part of the dignity of human work, the dignity of man, and the dignity of each and every worker in Australia!

And with the passing of each day may God give you an ever greater awareness of this dignity, and may he fill your lives and your homes with his peace and his joy.

**Right:** *Pope John Paul II pets Melinda, a year-old kangaroo, outside the Adelaide Festival Center after an address to rural industries, November 30, 1986. The pope expressed the desire to see a kangaroo so that he would know he was really in Australia.*

*Aboriginal dancers perform a traditional spiritual dance for Pope John Paul II at Rlatherskite park near Alice Springs, November 29, 1986.*

*Pope John Paul II waves to a cheering crowd today as he enters Munich's Olympic Stadium for the start of an outdoor Mass May 3, 1987. The Pope also beatified Father Rupert Meyer, a local priest who was interned during World War II by the Nazis.*

*Pope John Paul II shakes hands with U.S. President Ronald Reagan during their meeting at the Vatican June 6, 1987.*

***Right:*** *Solidarity leader Lech Walesa and wife Danuta kneel during a mass given by Pope John Paul II in Gdansk, Poland, June 12, 1987.*

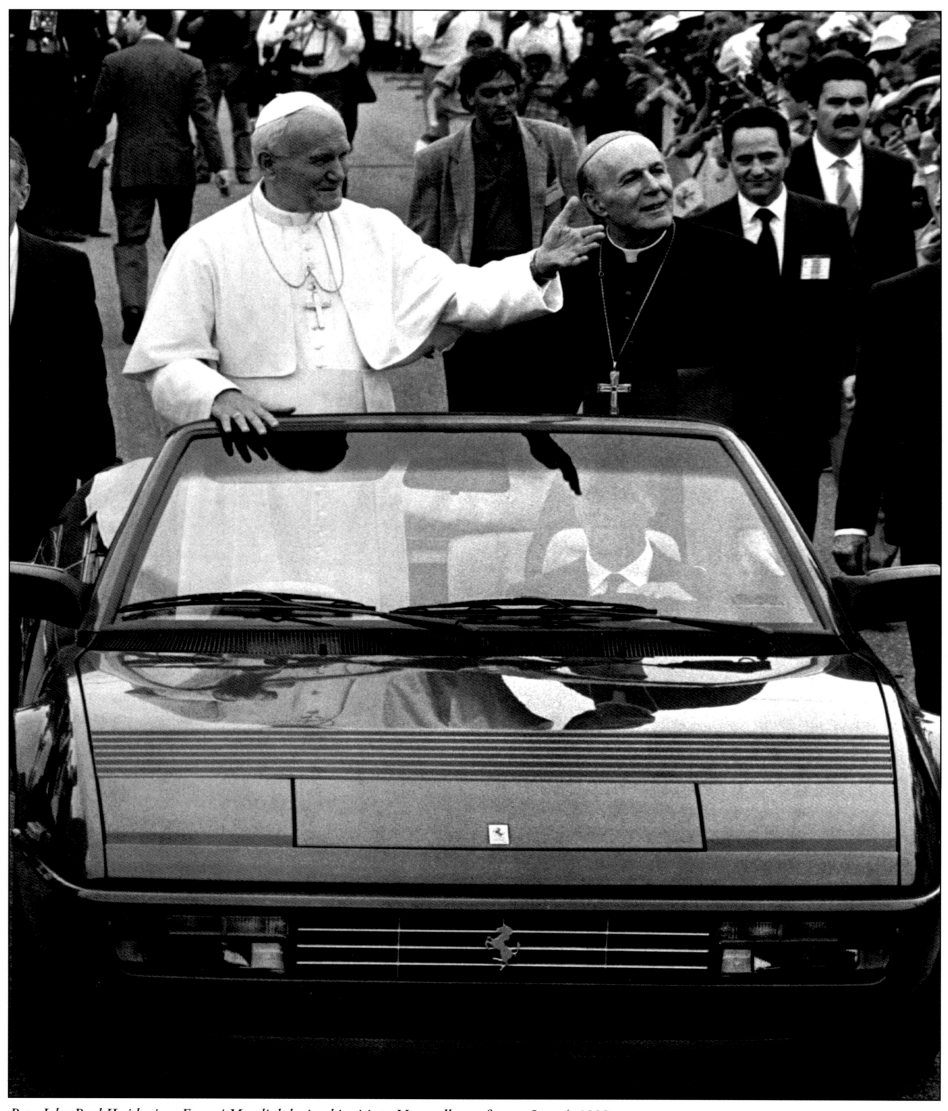

*Pope John Paul II rides in a Ferrari Mondial during his visit to Maranello car factory June 4, 1988.*

*Pope John Paul II arrives at Swaziland Somhlolo Stadium September 16, 1988 for a mass attended by some 12,000 people. The Pope is welcomed by a Swazi man dressed in traditional dress.*

*Pope John Paul II blesses one of 20 mutilated victims of Mozambique's civil war who attended an open-air mass in Beira, Mozambique, September 17, 1988.*

*Pope John Paul II touches hands with the crowd at Oropaa on July 16, 1989, during a private vacation of 10 days.*

***Right:*** *Pope John Paul II hugs three-year-old Monik and her one-year-old sister Zin, whose eye can be seen between the Pope's chest and hand, in Antananarivo, April 29, 1989. The two girls, dressed in rags, walked on the Pope's platform while he was addressing a youth rally in the capital of Madagascar.*

## ADDRESS OF JOHN PAUL II TO THE PRELATE AUDITORS, OFFICIALS AND ADVOCATES OF THE TRIBUNAL OF THE ROMAN ROTA

Monday, 28 January 2002

1. I cordially thank Monsignor Funghini, the Dean, who, while expressing your sentiments of respect and concern, explained your daily labour with comments and statistics that stress the serious and complex matters on which you must render a decision. The solemn inauguration of the new judicial year gives me the welcome chance for a cordial meeting with all those who carry out the mission of justice in the Tribunal of the Roman Rota - Prelate Auditors, Promoters of Justice, Defenders of the Bond, Officials and Advocates - to show them my appreciation, my esteem and encouragement. The administration of justice in the Christian community is a precious service, because it constitutes the indispensable premise for authentic charity.

Your judicial activity, as the Dean has stressed, is directed above all to causes of matrimonial annulment. On this subject, together with other ecclesiastical tribunals and with a special role among them, that I emphasized in Pastor Bonus (cf. art. 126), you constitute a particular institutional expression of the solicitude of the Church in judging, according to truth and justice, the delicate matter of whether or not a marriage exists. This mission of the tribunals in the Church, an indispensable contribution, belongs to the whole area of the pastoral service to marriage and family life. The pastoral aspect itself calls for the constant effort to develop more fully the truth about marriage and the family, even as a necessary condition for administering justice in this field.

2. The essential properties of marriage - unity and indissolubility (cf. CIC, can. 1056; CCEO, can. 776 3) - offer an opportunity for a fruitful reflection on marriage. Today, taking up what I treated last year in my discourse on indissolubility (cf. AAS, 92 [2000], pp. 350-355), I want to examine indissolublity as a good for spouses, for children, for the Church and for the whole of humanity.

A positive presentation of the indissoluble union is important, in order to rediscover its goodness and beauty. First of all, one must overcome the view of indissolubility as a restriction of the freedom of the contracting parties, and so as a burden that at times can become unbearable. Indissolubility, in this conception, is seen as a law that is extrinsic to marriage, as an "imposition" of a norm against the "legitimate" expectations of the further fulfilment of the person. Add to this the widespread notion that indissoluble marriage is only for believers, who cannot try to "impose" it on the rest of civil society.

3. To give a valid and complete response to this problem one must begin with the word of God. I am thinking concretely of the passage of the Gospel of Matthew that recounts Jesus' conversation about divorce with some Pharisees and then with his disciples (cf. Mt 19,3-12). Jesus goes radically beyond the debates of his day concerning the factors that could justify divorce asserting: "For your hardness of heart Moses allowed you to divorce your wives, but from the beginning it was not so" (Mt 19,8).

According to the teaching of Jesus, it is God who has joined man and woman together in the marital bond. Certainly this union takes place with the free consent of both parties, but this human consent concerns a plan that is divine. In other words, it is the natural dimension of the union and, more concretely, the nature of man created by God himself that provides the indispensable key for interpreting the essential properties of marriage. The farther reinforcement that the properties obtain in Christian marriage by virtue of the sacrament (cf. can. 1056) is based on a foundation of natural law that, if removed, would make incomprehensible the very work of salvation and elevation of the conjugal reality that Christ effected once and for all.

4. Countless men and women of all times and places have complied with this divine and natural plan, even before the Saviour's coming and a great many others have done so after his coming, even without knowing him. Their freedom expands to the gift of God, both at the moment of their marriage and throughout their entire conjugal life. Yet the possibility always exists of rebelling against that loving plan: then returns the "hardness of heart" that had led Moses to permit divorce but which Christ definitively overcame. To such situations as these, one has to respond with the humble courage of faith, a faith that supports and corroborates reason itself, to enable it to carry on a dialogue with all who are in search of the true good of the human person and of society. To treat indissolubility not as a natural juridical norm but as a mere ideal empties of meaning the unequivocal declaration of Jesus Christ, who absolutely refused divorce because "from the beginning it was not so" (Mt 19,8).

Marriage "is" indissoluble: this property expresses a dimension of its objective being, it is not a mere subjective fact. Consequently, the good of indissolubility is the good of marriage itself; and the lack of understanding of its indissoluble character constitutes the lack of understanding of the essence of marriage. It follows that the "burden" of indissolubility and the limits it entails for human freedom are no other than the reverse side of the coin with regard to the good and the potential inherent in the marital institution as such. In this perspective, it is meaningless to speak of an "imposition" by human law, because

human law should reflect and safeguard the natural and divine law, that is always a freeing truth (cf. Jn 8,32).

Pastoral care entails clarity about indissolubility and the support of marital love and communion

5. This truth about the indissolubility of marriage, like the entire Christian message, is addressed to the men and women of every time and place. In order to make that a reality, testimony to that truth must be given by the Church and, in particular, by individual families as "domestic Churches" in which husband and wife recognize that they are bound to each other forever by a bond that demands a love that is ever renewed, generous and ready for sacrifice.

One cannot give in to the divorce mentality: confidence in the natural and supernatural gifts of God to man prevents that. Pastoral activity must support and promote indissolubility. The doctrinal aspects should be transmitted, clarified and defended, but even more important are consistent actions. Whenever a couple is going through difficulties, the sympathy of Pastors, and of the other faithful must be combined with clarity and fortitude in remembering that conjugal love is the way to work out a positive solution to their crisis. Given that God has united them by means of an indissoluble bond, the husband and wife by utilizing all their human resources, together with good will, and by, above all, confiding in the assistance of divine grace, can and should emerge from their moments of crisis renewed and strengthened.

6. When one considers the role of law in marital crises, all too often one thinks almost exclusively of processes that ratify the annulment of marriage or the dissolution of the bond. At times, this mentality extends even to canon law, so that it appears as the avenue for resolving the marital problems of the faithful in a way that does not offend one's conscience. There is indeed some truth to this, but these eventual solutions must be examined in a way that the indissolubility of the bond, whenever it turns out to be validly contracted, continues to be safeguarded. The attitude of the Church is, in contrast, favourable to convalidating, where possible, marriages that are otherwise null (cf. CIC, can. 1676; CCEO, can. 1362). It is true that the declaration of the nullity of a marriage, based on the truth acquired by means of a legitimate process, restores peace to the conscience, but such a declaration - and the same holds true for the dissolution of a marriage that is ratum non consummatum or a dissolution based upon the privilege of the faith - must be presented and effected in an ecclesial context that is totally favourable to the indissolubility of marriage and to family founded upon it. The spouses themselves must be the first to realize that only in the loyal quest for the truth can they find their true good, without excluding a priori the possible convalidation of a union that, although it is not yet a sacramental marriage, contains elements of good, for themselves and their children, that should be carefully evaluated in conscience before reaching a different decision.

7. The judicial activity of the Church, which is always at the same time genuinely pastoral activity, draws its inspiration from the principle of the indissolubility of marriage and strives to guarantee its effective existence among the People of God. In effect, without the proceedings and sentences of ecclesiastical tribunals, the question of whether or not an indissoluble marriage exists would be relegated solely to the consciences of the faithful, with the evident risk of subjectivism, particularly when the civil society is experiencing a profound crisis concerning the institution of marriage.

Every correct judgement of the validity or nullity of a marriage contributes to the culture of indissolubility, in the Church and in the world. It is a very important and necessary contribution: indeed, it has an immediate practical application, since it gives certainty not only to the individual persons involved, but also to all marriages and families. Consequently, an unjust declaration of nullity, opposed to the truth of the normative principles or the facts, is particularly serious, since its official link with the Church encourages the spread of attitudes in which indissolubility finds verbal support, but is denied in practice.

At times, in recent years some have opposed the traditional "favor matrimonii" in the name of a "favor libertatis" or "favor personae". In this dialectic it is obvious that the basic theme is that of indissolubility, but the antithesis is even more radical with regard to the truth about marriage itself, more or less openly relativized. Against the truth of a conjugal bond, it is not right to invoke the freedom of the contracting parties, who, in freely consenting to that bond, were bound to respect the objective demands of the reality of marriage that cannot be altered in the name of human freedom. Judicial activity must therefore be inspired by a "favor indissolubilitatis"; that clearly does not mean prejudice against just declarations of nullity, but an active conviction of the good at stake in the processes, together with the ever renewed optimism that derives from the natural character of marriage and from the support of the Lord for the spouses.

8. The Church and every Christian must be the light of the world: "Let your light so shine before men, that they may see your good works and give glory to your Father who is in heaven" (Mt 5,16). Jesus' words have a special application today to the indissoluble nature of marriage. It could perhaps seem that divorce is so firmly rooted in certain social sectors that it is almost not worth continuing to combat it by spreading a mentality, a social custom and civil legislation in favour of the indissolubility of

marriage. Yet it is indeed worth the effort! Actually, this good is at the root of all society, as a necessary condition for the existence of the family. Its absence, therefore, has devastating consequences that spread through the social body like a plague - to use the term of the Second Vatican Council to describe divorce (cf. Gaudium et spes, n. 47) - and that have a negative influence on the new generations who view as tarnished the beauty of true marriage.

9. The essential witness to the value of indissolubility is given through the married life of the spouses, in their fidelity to the bond, through all the joys and trials of life. However the value of indissolubility cannot be held to be just the object of a private choice: it concerns one of the cornerstones of all society. Therefore, while all the initiatives that Christians, along with other persons of good will, promote for the good of the family (for example, the celebrations of wedding anniversaries) are to be encouraged, one must avoid the risk of permissiveness on fundamental issues concerning the nature of marriage and the family (cf. Letter to Families, n. 17).
Among the initiatives should be those that aim at obtaining the public recognition of indissoluble marriage in the civil juridical order (cf. ibid., n. 17). Resolute opposition to any legal or administrative measures that introduce divorce or that equate de facto unions–including those between homosexuals– with marriage must be accompanied by a pro-active attitude, acting through juridical provisions that tend to improve the social recognition of true marriage in the framework of legal orders that unfortunately admit divorce.
On the other hand, professionals in the field of civil law should avoid being personally involved in anything that might imply a cooperation with divorce. For judges this may prove difficult, since the legal order does not recognize a conscientious objection to exempt them from giving sentence.
For grave and proportionate motives they may therefore act in accord with the traditional principles of material cooperation. But they too must seek effective means to encourage marital unions, especially through a wisely handled work of reconciliation. Lawyers, as independent professionals, should always decline the use of their profession for an end that is contrary to justice, as is divorce. They can only cooperate in this kind of activity when, in the intention of the client, it is not directed to the break-up of the

marriage, but to the securing of other legitimate effects that can only be obtained through such a judicial process in the established legal order (cf. Catechism of the Catholic Church, n. 2383). In this way, with their work of assisting and reconciling persons who are going through a marital crises, lawyers truly serve the rights of the person and avoid becoming mere technicians at the service of any interest whatever.
10. I entrust to the intercession of Mary, Queen of the Family and Mirror of Justice, the heightening of everyone's conviction of the good of the indissolubility of marriage. To her I also entrust the zealous work of the Church and of her children, together with that of many other men and women of good will, in this cause that is so crucial for the future of humanity.
With these wishes, as I ask divine assistance on all your activities, Prelate Auditors, Officials and Advocates of the Roman Rota, I warmly impart my Blessing to you.

*Pope John Paul II blesses the many thousands of worshippers that attended the afternoon mass on the port of Prahia. Pope John Paul II blesses the many thousands of worshippers that attended the afternoon mass on the port of Prahia, January 26, 1990. The Pope ends his two-day visit to Cape Verde January 27, 1990.*

*Pope John Paul II meets Soviet leader Mikhail Gorbachev at a private audience at the Vatican November 18, 1990.*

*Pope John Paul II blesses the crowd after he was offered a feathered hat by an African Chief in Moundoun, Chad, January 31, 1990.*

*Above:* U.S. President George Bush applauds Pope John Paul II after the pope welcomed him to an audience in the Vatican following the Rome NATO summit, November 8, 1991.

*Right* Pope John Paul II waves as he leaves Rome's Gemelli hospital after major surgery in 1992.

*Overleaf:* Eleven bishops are prostrate in St. Peter's basilica in Vatican City in front of Pope John Paul II during their consecration January 6, 1992.

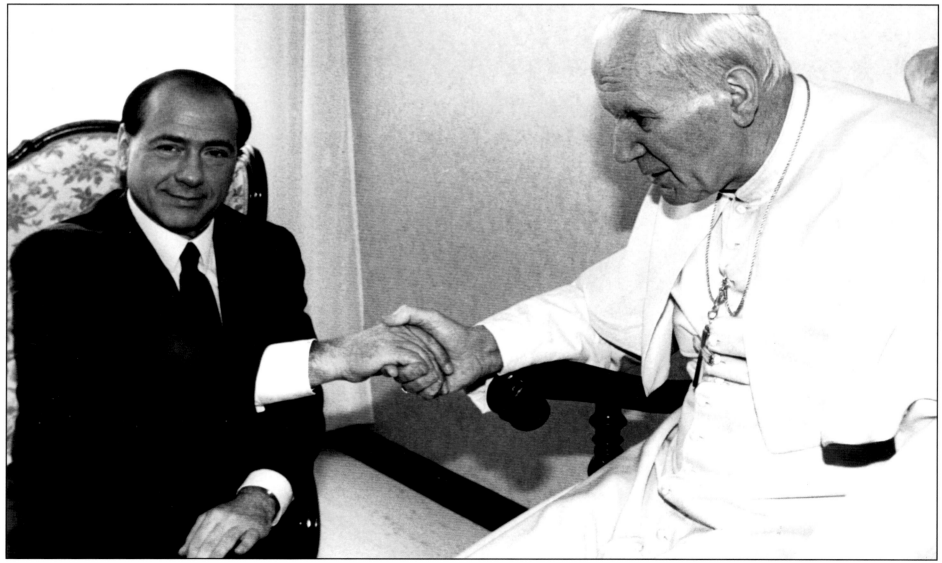

**Left Top:** *Pope John Paul II receives a gift from former Polish President Lech Walesa and his wife Danuta during an audience on May 19, 1994, at Rome's Gemelli hospital, where the Pope is recovering from surgery to repair a broken thigh bone.*

**Left Bottom:** *Prime Minister Silvio Berlusconi (L) shakes hands with Pope John Paul II at the Rome hospital where the Pontiff is recovering from leg surgery, May 21, 1994.*

**Below:** *South African President Nelson Mandela (R) and Pope John Paul II listen to national anthems after they met at Johannesburg International Airport September 16, 1995, at the start of the pope's first official visit to the country.*

*Singers John Secada (L) and Natalie Cole (R) perform before Pope John Paul II gave Mass on the Great Lawn in New York's Central Park October 7. Heavy overcast skies and a light rain greeted the crowd that was estimated at over 100,000 faithful.*

## ADDRESS OF HIS HOLINESS POPE JOHN PAUL II TO THE FIFTIETH GENERAL ASSEMBLY OF THE UNITED NATIONS ORGANIZATION

New York, October 5, 1995

*Mr. President,*
*Ladies and Gentlemen,*

1. It is an honour for me to have the opportunity to address this international Assembly and to join the men and women of every country, race, language and culture in celebrating the fiftieth anniversary of the founding of the United Nations Organization. In coming before this distinguished Assembly, I am vividly aware that through you I am in some way addressing the whole family of peoples living on the face of the earth. My words are meant as a sign of the interest and esteem of the Apostolic See and of the Catholic Church for this Institution. They echo the voices of all those who see in the United Nations the hope of a better future for human society.

I wish to express my heartfelt gratitude in the first place to the Secretary General, Dr. Boutros Boutros-Ghali, for having warmly encouraged this visit. And I thank you, Mr. President, for your cordial welcome. I greet all of you, the members of this General Assembly: I am grateful for your presence and for your kind attention.

I come before you today with the desire to be able to contribute to that thoughtful meditation on the history and role of this Organization which should accompany and give substance to the anniversary celebrations. The Holy See, in virtue of its specifically spiritual mission, which makes it concerned for the integral good of every human being, has supported the ideals and goals of the United Nations Organization from the very beginning. Although their respective purposes and operative approaches are obviously different, the Church and the United Nations constantly find wide areas of cooperation on the basis of their common concern for the human family. It is this awareness which inspires my thoughts today; they will not dwell on any particular social, political, or economic question; rather, I would like to reflect with you on what the extraordinary changes of the last few years imply, not simply for the present, but for the future of the whole human family.

*A Common Human Patrimony*

2. Ladies and Gentlemen! On the threshold of a new millennium we are witnessing an extraordinary global acceleration of that quest for freedom which is one of the great dynamics of human history. This phenomenon is not limited to any one part of the world; nor is it the expression of any single culture. Men and women throughout the world, even when threatened by violence, have taken the risk of freedom, asking to be given a place in social, political, and economic life which is commensurate with their dignity as free human beings. This universal longing for freedom is truly one of the distinguishing marks of our time.

During my previous Visit to the United Nations on 2 October 1979, I noted that the quest for freedom in our time has its basis in those universal rights which human beings enjoy by the very fact of their humanity. It was precisely outrages against human dignity which led the United Nations Organization to formulate, barely three years after its establishment, that Universal Declaration of Human Rights which remains one of the highest expressions of the human conscience of our time. In Asia and Africa, in the Americas, in Oceania and Europe, men and women of conviction and courage have appealed to this Declaration in support of their claims for a fuller share in the life of society.

3. It is important for us to grasp what might be called the inner structure of this worldwide movement. It is precisely its global character which offers us its first and fundamental "key" and confirms that there are indeed universal human rights, rooted in the nature of the person, rights which reflect the objective and inviolable demands of a universal moral law. These are not abstract points; rather, these rights tell us something important about the actual life of every individual and of every social group. They also remind us that we do not live in an irrational or meaningless world. On the contrary, there is a moral logic which is built into human life and which makes possible dialogue between individuals and peoples. If we want a century of violent coercion to be succeeded by a century of persuasion, we must find a way to discuss the human future intelligibly. The universal moral law written on the human heart is precisely that kind of "grammar" which is needed if the world is to engage this discussion of its future.

In this sense, it is a matter for serious concern that some people today deny the universality of human rights, just as they deny that there is a human nature shared by everyone. To be sure, there is no single model for organizing the politics and economics of human freedom; different cultures and different historical experiences give rise to different institutional forms of public life in a free and responsible society. But it is one thing to affirm a legitimate pluralism of "forms of freedom", and another to deny any

universality or intelligibility to the nature of man or to the human experience. The latter makes the international politics of persuasion extremely difficult, if not impossible.

*Taking the Risk of Freedom*

4. The moral dynamics of this universal quest for freedom clearly appeared in Central and Eastern Europe during the non-violent revolutions of 1989. Unfolding in specific times and places, those historical events nonetheless taught a lesson which goes far beyond a specific geographical location. For the non-violent revolutions of 1989 demonstrated that the quest for freedom cannot be suppressed. It arises from a recognition of the inestimable dignity and value of the human person, and it cannot fail to be accompanied by a commitment on behalf of the human person. Modern totalitarianism has been, first and foremost, an assault on the dignity of the person, an assault which has gone even to the point of denying the inalienable value of the individual's life. The revolutions of 1989 were made possible by the commitment of brave men and women inspired by a different, and ultimately more profound and powerful, vision: the vision of man as a creature of intelligence and free will, immersed in a mystery which transcends his own being and endowed with the ability to reflect and the ability to choose — and thus capable of wisdom and virtue. A decisive factor in the success of those non-violent revolutions was the experience of social solidarity: in the face of regimes backed by the power of propaganda and terror, that solidarity was the moral core of the "power of the powerless", a beacon of hope and an enduring reminder that it is possible for man's historical journey to follow a path which is true to the finest aspirations of the human spirit.

Viewing those events from this privileged international forum, one cannot fail to grasp the connection between the values which inspired those people's liberation movements and many of the moral commitments inscribed in the United Nations Charter: I am thinking for example of the commitment to "reaffirm faith in fundamental human rights (and) in the dignity and worth of the human person"; and also the commitment "to promote social progress and better standards of life in larger freedom" (Preamble). The fifty-one States which founded this Organization in 1945 truly lit a lamp whose light can scatter the darkness caused by tyranny — a light which can show the way to freedom, peace, and solidarity.

*The Rights of Nations*

5. The quest for freedom in the second half of the twentieth century has engaged not only individuals but nations as well. Fifty years after the end of the Second World War, it is important to remember that that war was fought because of violations of the rights of nations. Many of those nations suffered grievously for no other reason than that they were deemed "other". Terrible crimes were committed in the name of lethal doctrines which taught the "inferiority" of some nations and cultures. In a certain sense, the United Nations Organization was born from a conviction that such doctrines were antithetical to peace; and the Charter's commitment to "save future generations from the scourge of war" (Preamble) surely implied a moral commitment to defend every nation and culture from unjust and violent aggression.

Unfortunately, even after the end of the Second World War, the rights of nations continued to be violated. To take but one set of examples, the Baltic States and extensive territories in Ukraine and Belarus were absorbed into the Soviet Union, as had already happened to Armenia, Azerbaijan, and Georgia in the Caucasus. At the same time the so-called "People's Democracies" of Central and Eastern Europe effectively lost their sovereignty and were required to submit to the will dominating the entire bloc. The result of this artificial division of Europe was the "cold war", a situation of international tension in which the threat of a nuclear holocaust hung over humanity. It was only when freedom was restored to the nations of Central and Eastern Europe that the promise of the peace which should have come with the end of the war began to be realized for many of the victims of that conflict.

6. The Universal Declaration of Human Rights, adopted in 1948, spoke eloquently of the rights of persons; but no similar international agreement has yet adequately addressed the rights of nations. This situation must be carefully pondered, for it raises urgent questions about justice and freedom in the world today.

In reality the problem of the full recognition of the rights of peoples and nations has presented itself repeatedly to the conscience of humanity, and has also given rise to considerable ethical and juridical reflection. I am reminded of the debate which took place at the Council of Constance in the fifteenth century, when the representatives of the Academy of Krakow, headed by Pawel Włodkowic, courageously defended the right of certain European peoples to existence and independence. Still better known is the discussion which went on in that same period at the University of Salamanca with regard to the peoples of the New World. And in our own century, how can I fail to mention the prophetic words of my predecessor, Pope Benedict XV, who in the midst of the First World War reminded everyone that "nations do not die", and invited them "to ponder with serene conscience the rights and the just aspirations of peoples" (To the Peoples at War and their Leaders, 28 July 1915)?

*Pope John Paul II speaks before the 50th General Assembly at the United Nations in New York October 5, 1995. The Pope urged the United Nations to rise above its status as an administrative body and become a moral center for the world.*

7. Today the problem of nationalities forms part of a new world horizon marked by a great "mobility" which has blurred the ethnic and cultural frontiers of the different peoples, as a result of a variety of processes such as migrations, mass-media and the globalization of the economy. And yet, precisely against this horizon of universality we see the powerful re-emergence of a certain ethnic and cultural consciousness, as it were an explosive need for identity and survival, a sort of counterweight to the tendency toward uniformity. This is a phenomenon which must not be underestimated or regarded as a simple left-over of the past. It demands serious interpretation, and a closer examination on the levels of anthropology, ethics and law.

This tension between the particular and the universal can be considered immanent in human beings. By virtue of sharing in the same human nature, people automatically feel that they are members of one great family, as is in fact the case. But as a result of the concrete historical conditioning of this same nature, they are necessarily bound in a more intense way to particular human groups, beginning with the family and going on to the various groups to which they belong and up to the whole of their ethnic and cultural group, which is called, not by accident, a "nation", from the Latin word "nasci": "to be born". This term, enriched with another one, "patria" (fatherland/motherland), evokes the reality of the family. The human condition thus finds itself between these two poles — universality and particularity — with a vital tension between them; an inevitable tension, but singularly fruitful if they are lived in a calm and balanced way.

8. Upon this anthropological foundation there also rest the "rights of nations", which are nothing but "human rights" fostered at the specific level of community life. A study of these rights is certainly not easy, if we consider the difficulty of defining the very concept of "nation", which cannot be identified a priori and necessarily with the State. Such a study must nonetheless be made, if we wish to avoid the errors of the past and ensure a just world order.

A presupposition of a nation's rights is certainly its right to exist: therefore no one — neither a State nor another nation, nor an international organization — is ever justified in asserting that an individual nation is not worthy of existence. This fundamental right to existence does not necessarily call for sovereignty as a state, since various forms of juridical aggregation between different nations are possible, as for example occurs in Federal States, in Confederations or in States characterized by broad regional autonomies. There can be historical circumstances in which aggregations different from single state sovereignty can even prove advisable, but only on condition that this takes place in a climate of true freedom, guaranteed by the exercise of the self-determination of the peoples concerned. Its right to exist naturally implies that every nation also enjoys the right to its own language and culture, through which a people expresses and promotes that which I would call its fundamental spiritual "sovereignty". History shows that in extreme circumstances (such as those which occurred in the land where I was born) it is precisely its culture that enables a nation to survive the loss of political and economic independence. Every nation therefore has also the right to shape its life according to its own traditions, excluding, of course, every abuse of basic human rights and in particular the oppression of minorities. Every nation has the right to build its future by providing an appropriate education for the younger generation.

But while the "rights of the nation" express the vital requirements of "particularity", it is no less important to emphasize the requirements of universality, expressed through a clear awareness of the duties which nations have vis-à-vis other nations and humanity as a whole. Foremost among these duties is certainly that of living in a spirit of peace, respect and solidarity with other nations. Thus the exercise of the rights of nations, balanced by the acknowledgement and the practice of duties, promotes a fruitful "exchange of gifts", which strengthens the unity of all mankind.

### Respect for Differences

9. During my pastoral pilgrimages to the communities of the Catholic Church over the past seventeen years, I have been able to enter into dialogue with the rich diversity of nations and cultures in every part of the world. Unhappily, the world has yet to learn how to live with diversity, as recent events in the Balkans and Central Africa have painfully reminded us. The fact of "difference", and the reality of "the other", can sometimes be felt as a burden, or even as a threat. Amplified by historic grievances and exacerbated by the manipulations of the unscrupulous, the fear of "difference" can lead to a denial of the very humanity of "the other": with the result that people fall into a cycle of violence in which no one is spared, not even the children. We are all very familiar today with such situations; at this moment my heart and my prayers turn in a special way to the sufferings of the sorely tried peoples of Bosnia-Hercegovina.

From bitter experience, then, we know that the fear of "difference", especially when it expresses itself in a narrow and exclusive nationalism which denies any rights to "the other", can lead to a true nightmare of violence and terror. And yet if we make the effort to look at matters objectively, we can see that, transcending all the differences which distinguish individuals and peoples, there is a fundamental commonality. For different cultures are but different ways of facing the question of the meaning of personal existence. And it is precisely here that we find one source of the respect which is due to every culture and every nation: every culture is an effort to ponder the mystery of the world and in particular of the human person: it is a way of giving expression to the transcendent

dimension of human life. The heart of every culture is its approach to the greatest of all mysteries: the mystery of God.

10. Our respect for the culture of others is therefore rooted in our respect for each community's attempt to answer the question of human life. And here we can see how important it is to safeguard the fundamental right to freedom of religion and freedom of conscience, as the cornerstones of the structure of human rights and the foundation of every truly free society. No one is permitted to suppress those rights by using coercive power to impose an answer to the mystery of man.

To cut oneself off from the reality of difference — or, worse, to attempt to stamp out that difference — is to cut oneself off from the possibility of sounding the depths of the mystery of human life. The truth about man is the unchangeable standard by which all cultures are judged; but every culture has something to teach us about one or other dimension of that complex truth. Thus the "difference" which some find so threatening can, through respectful dialogue, become the source of a deeper understanding of the mystery of human existence.

11. In this context, we need to clarify the essential difference between an unhealthy form of nationalism, which teaches contempt for other nations or cultures, and patriotism, which is a proper love of one's country. True patriotism never seeks to advance the well-being of one's own nation at the expense of others. For in the end this would harm one's own nation as well: doing wrong damages both aggressor and victim. Nationalism, particularly in its most radical forms, is thus the antithesis of true patriotism, and today we must ensure that extreme nationalism does not continue to give rise to new forms of the aberrations of totalitarianism. This is a commitment which also holds true, obviously, in cases where religion itself is made the basis of nationalism, as unfortunately happens in certain manifestations of so-called "fundamentalism".

### Freedom and Moral Truth

12. Ladies and Gentlemen! Freedom is the measure of man's dignity and greatness. Living the freedom sought by individuals and peoples is a great challenge to man's spiritual growth and to the moral vitality of nations. The basic question which we must all face today is the responsible use of freedom, in both its personal and social dimensions. Our reflection must turn then to the question of the moral structure of freedom, which is the inner architecture of the culture of freedom.

Freedom is not simply the absence of tyranny or oppression. Nor is freedom a licence to do whatever we like. Freedom has an inner "logic" which distinguishes it and ennobles it: freedom is ordered to the truth, and is fulfilled in man's quest for truth and in man's living in the truth. Detached from the truth about the human person, freedom deteriorates into license in the lives of individuals, and, in political life, it becomes the caprice of the most powerful and the arrogance of power. Far from being a limitation upon freedom or a threat to it, reference to the truth about the human person — a truth universally knowable through the moral law written on the hearts of all — is, in fact, the guarantor of freedom's future.

13. In the light of what has been said we understand how utilitarianism, the doctrine which defines morality not in terms of what is good but of what is advantageous, threatens the freedom of individuals and nations and obstructs the building of a true culture of freedom. Utilitarianism often has devastating political consequences, because it inspires an aggressive nationalism on the basis of which the subjugation, for example, of a smaller or weaker nation is claimed to be a good thing solely because it corresponds to the national interest. No less grave are the results of economic utilitarianism, which drives more powerful countries to manipulate and exploit weaker ones.

Nationalistic and economic utilitarianism are sometimes combined, a phenomenon which has too often characterized relations between the "North" and the "South". For the emerging countries, the achievement of political independence has too frequently been accompanied by a situation of de facto economic dependence on other countries; indeed, in some cases, the developing world has suffered a regression, such that some countries lack the means of satisfying the essential needs of their people. Such situations offend the conscience of humanity and pose a formidable moral challenge to the human family. Meeting this challenge will obviously require changes in both developing and developed countries. If developing countries are able to offer sure guarantees of the proper management of resources and of assistance received, as well as respect for human rights, by replacing where necessary unjust, corrupt, or authoritarian forms of government with participatory and democratic ones, will they not in this way unleash the best civil and economic energies of their people? And must not the developed countries, for their part, come to renounce strictly utilitarian approaches and develop new approaches inspired by greater justice and solidarity?

Yes, distinguished Ladies and Gentlemen! The international economic scene needs an ethic of solidarity, if participation, economic growth, and a just distribution of goods are to characterize the future of humanity. The international cooperation called for by the Charter of the United Nations for "solving international problems of an economic, social, cultural, or humanitarian character" (art. 1.3) cannot be conceived exclusively in terms of help and assistance, or even by considering the eventual returns on the resources provided. When millions of people are suffering from a poverty which means hunger, malnutrition, sickness, illiteracy, and degradation, we must not only remind ourselves that no one has a right to exploit another for his own advantage, but also and above all we must recommit ourselves to that solidarity which enables others to live out, in the actual circumstances of their economic and political lives, the creativity which is a distinguishing mark of the human person and the true source of the wealth of nations in today's world.

*The United Nations and the Future of Freedom*

14. As we face these enormous challenges, how can we fail to acknowledge the role of the United Nations Organization? Fifty years after its founding, the need for such an Organization is even more obvious, but we also have a better understanding, on the basis of experience, that the effectiveness of this great instrument for harmonizing and coordinating international life depends on the international culture and ethic which it supports and expresses. The United Nations Organization needs to rise more and more above the cold status of an administrative institution and to become a moral centre where all the nations of the world feel at home and develop a shared awareness of being, as it were, a "family of nations". The idea of "family" immediately evokes something more than simple functional relations or a mere convergence of interests. The family is by nature a community based on mutual trust, mutual support and sincere respect. In an authentic family the strong do not dominate; instead, the weaker members, because of their very weakness, are all the more welcomed and served.
Raised to the level of the "family of nations", these sentiments ought to be, even before law itself, the very fabric of relations between peoples. The United Nations has the historic, even momentous, task of promoting this qualitative leap in international life, not only by serving as a centre of effective mediation for the resolution of conflicts but also by fostering values, attitudes and concrete initiatives of solidarity which prove capable of raising the level of relations between nations from the "organizational" to a more "organic" level, from simple "existence with" others to "existence for" others, in a fruitful exchange of gifts, primarily for the good of the weaker nations but even so, a clear harbinger of greater good for everyone.

15. Only on this condition shall we attain an end not only to "wars of combat" but also to "cold wars". It will ensure not only the legal equality of all peoples but also their active participation in the building of a better future, and not only respect for individual cultural identities, but full esteem for them as a common treasure belonging to the cultural patrimony of mankind. Is this not the ideal held up by the Charter of the United Nations when it sets as the basis of the Organization "the principle of the sovereign equality of all its Members" (art. 2.1), or when it commits it to "develop friendly relations between nations based on respect for the principle of equal rights and of self-determination" (art. 1.2)? This is the high road which must be followed to the end, even if this involves, when necessary, appropriate modifications in the operating model of the United Nations, so as to take into account everything that has happened in this half century, with so many new peoples experiencing freedom and legitimately aspiring to "be" and to "count for" more.
None of this should appear an unattainable utopia. Now is the time for new hope, which calls us to expel the paralyzing burden of cynicism from the future of politics and of human life. The anniversary which we are celebrating invites us to do this by reminding us of the idea of "united nations", an idea which bespeaks mutual trust, security and solidarity. Inspired by the example of all those who have taken the risk of freedom, can we not recommit ourselves also to taking the risk of solidarity — and thus the risk of peace?

*Beyond Fear: the Civilization of Love*

16. It is one of the great paradoxes of our time that man, who began the period we call "modernity" with a self-confident assertion of his "coming of age" and "autonomy", approaches the end of the twentieth century fearful of himself, fearful of what he might be capable of, fearful for the future. Indeed, the second half of the twentieth century has seen the unprecedented phenomenon of a humanity uncertain about the very likelihood of a future, given the threat of nuclear war. That danger, mercifully, appears to have receded — and everything that might make it return needs to be rejected firmly and universally; all the same, fear for the future and of the future remains.
In order to ensure that the new millennium now approaching will witness a new flourishing of the human spirit, mediated through an authentic culture of freedom, men and women must learn to conquer fear. We must learn not to be afraid, we must rediscover a spirit of hope and a spirit of trust. Hope is not empty optimism springing from a naive confidence that the future will necessarily be better than the past. Hope and trust are the premise of responsible activity and are nurtured in that inner sanctuary of conscience where "man is alone with God" (Gaudium et Spes, 16) and he thus perceives that he is not alone amid the enigmas of existence, for he is surrounded by the love of the Creator!
Hope and trust: these may seem matters beyond the purview of the United Nations.

But they are not. The politics of nations, with which your Organization is principally concerned, can never ignore the transcendent, spiritual dimension of the human experience, and could never ignore it without harming the cause of man and the cause of human freedom. Whatever diminishes man — whatever shortens the horizon of man's aspiration to goodness — harms the cause of freedom. In order to recover our hope and our trust at the end of this century of sorrows, we must regain sight of that transcendent horizon of possibility to which the soul of man aspires.

17. As a Christian, my hope and trust are centered on Jesus Christ, the two thousandth anniversary of whose birth will be celebrated at the coming of the new millennium. We Christians believe that in his Death and Resurrection were fully revealed God's love and his care for all creation. Jesus Christ is for us God made man, and made a part of the history of humanity. Precisely for this reason, Christian hope for the world and its future extends to every human person. Because of the radiant humanity of Christ, nothing genuinely human fails to touch the hearts of Christians. Faith in Christ does not impel us to intolerance. On the contrary, it obliges us to engage others in a respectful dialogue. Love of Christ does not distract us from interest in others, but rather invites us to responsibility for them, to the exclusion of no one and indeed, if anything, with a special concern for the weakest and the suffering. Thus, as we approach the two thousandth anniversary of the birth of Christ, the Church asks only to be able to propose respectfully this message of salvation, and to be able to promote, in charity and service, the solidarity of the entire human family.
Ladies and Gentlemen! I come before you, as did my predecessor Pope Paul VI exactly thirty years ago, not as one who exercises temporal power — these are his words — nor as a religious leader seeking special privileges for his community. I come before you as a witness: a witness to human dignity, a witness to hope, a witness to the conviction that the destiny of all nations lies in the hands of a merciful Providence.

18. We must overcome our fear of the future. But we will not be able to overcome it completely unless we do so together. The "answer" to that fear is neither coercion nor repression, nor the imposition of one social "model" on the entire world. The answer to the fear which darkens human existence at the end of the twentieth century is the common effort to build the civilization of love, founded on the universal values of peace, solidarity, justice, and liberty. And the "soul" of the civilization of love is the culture of freedom: the freedom of individuals and the freedom of nations, lived in self-giving solidarity and responsibility.
We must not be afraid of the future. We must not be afraid of man. It is no accident that we are here. Each and every human person has been created in the "image and likeness" of the One who is the origin of all that is. We have within us the capacities for wisdom and virtue. With these gifts, and with the help of God's grace, we can build in the next century and the next millennium a civilization worthy of the human person, a true culture of freedom. We can and must do so! And in doing so, we shall see that the tears of this century have prepared the ground for a new springtime of the human spirit.

**Right:** *Pope John Paul II holds a crucifix against his head as he listens to the liturgy during the Mass on the great lawn in Central Park, October 7, 1995.*

**Overleaf:** *Pope John Paul II waves to the crowd at the end of his Mass at Aqueduct Raceway October 6, 1995, in Queens borough, New York. The Pope is on the 3rd day of a 5 day visit to the United States.*

*Above:* Pope John Paul II (C) and Dutch Bishops praying around the recently restored altar during a ceremony in Saint Clement and Magnus Church on November 12, 1995.

*Right:* A view of St. Peter's Basilica during solemn mass to open a special synod of the Catholic Church in Lebanon November 26, 1995.
Pope John Paul II presides at the central altar during the solemn mass.

*Left Top: Yitzak Rabin's widow Leah (L) poses with Pope John Paul II during a private audience at the Vatican December 14, 1995. Pope John Paul told Leah Rabin that her husband died a martyr for peace and repeated his intention to visit the Jewish state.*

*Left Bottom: A view of St. Peter's Basilica in which Pope John Paul II read a message for the Catholic Church's World Day of Peace January 1, 1996. The Pope greeted the world wishing everyone a 'happy and peaceful' New Year and called for children to be protected from violence.*

*Below: Pope John Paul II waves to the people below as he stands in the central loggia of St. Peter's Basilica April 7, 1996 to read his 'Urbi et Orbi' message. The Pope prayed for a victory over death in Bosnia, Ireland, the Middle East, Algeria and the world's other trouble spots.*

**Left:** *Pope John Paul II stands in front of the Berlin Brandenburg Gate together with German Chancellor Helmut Kohl (R), Berlin's Cardinal Georg Sterzinsky (far right) and Berlin's major Eberhard Diepgen (L), June 23, 1996. Pope John Paul II finished his three-day visit to Germany by walking through the symbol of the re-united Germany.*

**Above:** *Pope John Paul II (R) receives a book from Patrick Kennedy, the nephew of President John Kennedy during a private audience at the Vatican on July 1, 1996. The Pope paid tribute to the 19 American servicemen killed by a blast in Saudi Arabia, saying they had died defending freedom.*

*Pope John Paul II looks at the view during his holidays in the Italian Dolomiti mountains July 15, 1996.*

Pope John Paul II (R) greets the faithful gathered in Pieve di Cadore, northern Italy, at the end of his Angelus prayer and the last of his two public appearances during his private mountain holiday July 21, 1996. The Pope prayed for a peaceful Olympics and said his thoughts were with the families of 230 people killed this week when TWA Flight 800 mysteriously blew up soon after take-off from New York. On the left is Bishop Pietro Brollo.

*Right:* Pope John Paul II waves at wellwishers as he leaves Reims airbase after celebrating an open-air mass, September 22, 1996. Pope John Paul II is in France on the last day of a four-day visit.

*Israeli singer Rinat Gibai (R) performs in St. Peter's Square during the last day of ceremonies which marks Pope John Paul II 50 years as a priest. More than 1,500 Roman Catholic priests and 200 cardinals and bishops from around the world paid homage to the 76-year-old Pope.*

*Pope John Paul II is applauded after giving the opening speech of the World Food Summit November 13, 1996. The Pontiff called on world leaders to bridge the gulf between rich and poor telling the U.N. Food and Agricultural Organisation (FAO) sponsored summit it was intolerable that some people lived in opulence while others starved. Delegates at the summit adopted a plan aimed at halving the number of people who suffer chronic hunger and malnutrition from the present 840 million by the year 2015.*

*Cuban President Fidel Castro (L) meets Pope John Paul II during their private audience at the Vatican, November 19, 1996. They met for the first time at this historic Vatican audience that could pave the way for a papal trip to communist Cuba.*

*Holiness Karekin I Supreme Patriarch and Catholicos of All Armenians (L) gestures to Pope John Paul during their meeting at the Vatican December 13, 1996. His Holiness Kareken I, spiritual leader of the world's some six million Armenian Christians, is on a five-day official visit. The Armenian Church is one of the so-called Ancient Churches of the East which split away from Byzantine Christianity before the Great Schism of 1054.*

*Pope John Paul II (R) receives a gift from Kuwait's Crown Prince and Prime Minister Sheikh Saad al-Abdulla al-Sabah during their private audience at the Vatican December 13. It was the first such high-level meeting since 1969, when Kuwait became the first Gulf Arab state to establish diplomatic ties with the Vatican.*

*Left: A view of St. Peter's Basilica during the celebration of a solemn midnight mass held by Pope John Paul II December 24, 1996. The Pope led the world's some 960 million Roman Catholics into Christmas and said he prayed that the season would bring peace and joy to believers and non-believers alike.*

## HOMILY - MIDNIGHT MASS

24 December 1996

1. "In the depths of the night a voice resounds" (Polish Christmas carol). In the first reading the Prophet Isaiah says: "The people who walked in darkness have seen a great light; on those who dwelt in a land of deep darkness, on them has light shined" (Is 9:1). The light shone because "to us a child is born, to us a son is given" (Is 9:5). The same Christmas carol identifies that voice in the night: "Come, shepherds, God is born for you; hasten to Bethlehem to greet the Lord". It is the same voice which resounds in the passage of the Gospel of Luke just proclaimed: "In that region there were shepherds out in the fields keeping watch over their flock by night. And an angel of the Lord appeared to them, and the glory of the Lord shone around them, and they were filled with fear. The angel said to them, 'Be not afraid; for behold I bring you good news of a great joy which will come to all the people. For to you is born this day in the city of David a Saviour, who is Christ the Lord. And this will be a sign for you: you will find a babe wrapped in swaddling cloths and lying in a manger'" (Lk 2:8-12). The Christmas carol continues: "[The shepherds] set off, and in the manger they found the Child with all the signs which had foretold his birth. They adored him as God...".

2. What St Luke wrote in the Gospel about the birth of the Lord Jesus has been translated into countless songs and works of literature; these make up the rich tradition inspired by Christmas. We bring this tradition with us when we come to Midnight Mass, also called the "Mass of the Shepherds". At this hour, Bishops and priests throughout the world join me, the Bishop of Rome, in celebrating this Mass. In every place liturgical and extra-liturgical songs are proclaiming the joy of the Lord's birth. The angel says: Be not afraid, rejoice! The birth of a human being is always a source of great rejoicing (cf Jn 16:21). What great joy then must the birth of the God-Man bring! Isaiah says: "They rejoice before you as with joy at the harvest" (Is 9:2). A remarkable harvest! Behold, humanity is ripe for this moment when the Creator is born "of woman". Man, created in the image and likeness of God (cf. Gen 1:27), grows and journeys towards this God-Man, in whom he receives the gift of his own fulfilment and in whom, at the same time, all creation is raised to its fullness. The responsorial psalm of this liturgy proclaims: "Sing to the Lord a new song; sing to the Lord all the earth! Sing to the Lord, bless his name; tell of his salvation from day to day" (Ps 96:1-2). And a Christmas carol echoes: "Let all creation sing to its Lord". This invitation to praise resounds with particular eloquence. Behold: all creation, which the Apostle Paul will describe as "waiting with eager longing for the revealing of the sons of God" (Rom 8:19), becomes a witness of the revelation of the Son of God in human flesh. At the same time, this is the beginning and the foundation of the revelation of those who have become sons and daughters of God by reason of the divine adoption to which all people are called. What profound reasons for joy the Lord's birth gives us!

3. St Paul also speaks of these reasons in the Second Reading: "The grace of God has appeared for the salvation of all men" (Ti 2:11). The Son of God does not come into the world empty-handed. It is true that in the stable at Bethlehem he receives the gifts of the shepherds, but first he himself brings great gifts. His generosity is indescribable: "The loving Father offers us today ineffable gifts from heaven, as the Eternal Word becomes flesh, by his wondrous power" (Christmas carol). Precisely that priceless gift which the Apostle calls "grace" — the gift of a share in the life of God, a universal gift, the opening of the path of eternal salvation — is the most profound source of Christmas joy. With this joy in our hearts, we celebrate the solemn and beautiful night liturgy. We wish to join the choirs of angels who over the stable of Bethlehem are glorifying the Lord: "Glory to God in the highest, and on earth peace among men with whom he is pleased!" (Lk 2:14). We pray today for everyone, Christians and non-Christians, believers and non-believers alike. For we want to be faithful to the gift brought by God on Christmas night: the grace of our Lord Jesus Christ, made manifest for all humanity. From this Basilica of St Peter's, I send everyone a cordial greeting and I pray that this source of joy issuing forth in human history with the birth of the Son of God will be plentiful for all, so that each person may draw from it and quench his thirst. Yes, the fountain of salvation which God desires to offer to each human being has now been opened. It was for this very reason that he drew near to us and in his Son became like us: true God and true Man.

"God is born, man's might is amazed. The Lord of heaven empties himself! The fire subsides, the splendour is veiled, the Infinite is encompassed" (F. Karpiński, Christmas Song). On this night the frontiers of human existence are extended. The Son of God, taking upon himself man's limitations, opens before our eyes the prospect of God's infinity.

"Natus est hodie Salvator mundi".

Today is born the Saviour of the world.

Come, let us adore him!

*Pope John Paul blesses pilgrims in St. Peter's Square during his Urbi et Orbi (to the city and the world) message December 25, 1996. The Pontiff wished the world a happy Christmas in 55 languages but said the spirit of nativity was marred by tensions in the Holy Land and international indifference to the tragedy in Africa.*

*Mother Teresa of Calcutta (L) meets Pope John Paul II at the end of a service in St. Peter's Basilica on June 29, 1997, to mark the feast of the apostles Peter and Paul, who brought Christianity to Rome and were both martyred there during Roman persecutions. Pope John Paul has granted special dispensation from the Catholic Church rules that will allow Mother Teresa to be put on the track towards eventual sainthood more quickly, the Vatican said on Monday.*

*Pope John Paul II (R) looks at the relics of St Therese of Lisieux while people through red and white rose petals on it at the Vatican October 19, 1997. The Pope elevated St Therese of Lisieux, the humble French saint who inspired Mother Theresa to a lifetime of devotion, to a privileged place in the male-dominated Roman Catholic Church. The Pontiff pronounced the child nun, who died 100 years ago aged 24, a Doctor of the Church, a rank reserved for a handful of saints whose spirituality has deeply influenced the life of the Church and who are deemed some of its best teachers.*

*Pope John Paul II enters St. Peter's Square to preside over a solemn beatification ceremony November 9, 1997. The Pope put three people on the road to sainthood in the Roman Catholic Church, including Vilmos Apor, a Hungarian bishop who resisted Nazi attempts to exterminate the Jews in World War II.*

*U.S. blues legend B.B. King (L) gives his beloved electric guitar Lucille to Pope John Paul II during their meeting at the Vatican December 18, 1997. The 72-year-old artist handed over the guitar, his faithful touring companion of some 50 years, at a star-studded Papal audience for singers and musicians performing in the Vatican's upcoming 5th annual Christmas concert on December 19. The Pope handed B.B. King a small cross as a gift from the Vatican.*

**Right:** *Pope John Paul II (2nd from R) poses with Caroline of Monaco (L), Prince Rainier of Monaco and Alberto during a private meeting at the Vatican December 19, 1997. The Prince with his children Alberto and Caroline will attend the Christmas concert at the Vatican late in the evening.*

*The new Chilean cardinal Jorge Arturo Medina Estevez (R) receives the ring of office from Pope John Paul II during a solemn mass in St. Peter's Square February 22, 1998. The Pope addressing a new batch of cardinals who eventually will choose his successor, said he hoped the third Millennium of Christianity would launch a springtime of hope for humanity.*

## PASTORAL VISIT TO NIGERIA ARRIVAL AT NNAMDI AZIKIWE AIRPORT ADDRESS OF JOHN PAUL II

Saturday, 21 March 1998

Your Excellency the Head of State, General Sani Abacha,
Government Leaders,
My Brother Bishops,
Dear Brothers and Sisters in Christ Jesus,
Beloved People of Nigeria,

1. With profound gratitude I praise Divine Providence for granting me the grace of returning to you and of setting foot once more on this blessed land! To you who have gathered to welcome me, and to all the sons and daughters of Nigeria, I offer heartfelt greetings of love and peace.
I address a special word of gratitude to my Brother Bishops for their invitation, and to the Head of State, as well as to the other Government leaders and authorities, for making this Visit possible. I see the presence of all of you here today as a sign of friendship and a manifestation of your desire to work together to serve the well-being of the entire nation.

2. I come to Nigeria as a friend, as one who is deeply concerned for the destiny of your country and of Africa as a whole. The main purpose of my Visit is to celebrate with the Catholic community the Beatification of Father Cyprian Michael Iwene Tansi, the first Nigerian in the Church's history to be officially proclaimed "Blessed".
This Beatification in the very land where Father Tansi was born and exercised his priestly ministry honours the whole nation of Nigeria. It gives to all Nigerians an opportunity to reflect on the direction and insight which the life of Father Tansi provides for today's society. In him, and in all who dedicate their lives completely to the service of others, is revealed the path along which Nigerians should travel towards a brighter future for their country. The testimony borne by Father Tansi is important at this moment in Nigeria's history, a moment that requires concerted and honest efforts to foster harmony and national unity, to guarantee respect for human life and human rights, to promote justice and development, to combat unemployment, to give hope to the poor and the suffering, to resolve conflicts through dialogue and to establish a true and lasting solidarity between all sectors of society.

3. Violence has not ceased to bring great pain and torment to certain peoples of Africa. Arriving in West Africa, my thoughts turn to the people of Sierra Leone, who have suffered so much in recent times. We must all hope that, with the continuing help of those responsible for peace in Africa, the return to constitutional order and democratic freedom will open the way to a new period of reconstruction and development.
In this respect I duly recognize the contributions made by Nigeria and other countries to help in this difficult situation. In particular I wish to express my sincere gratitude to all those who cooperated in the successful rescue operation at the Catholic Pastoral Centre in Makeni.
I wish also to encourage the people of Liberia as they come out of a situation of tragic conflict and work to rebuild their nation. Justice and peace are the path of development and progress. May God strengthen those who walk this path in the service of the human community.

4. Dear Nigerian Friends, in your own country you are all called to muster your wisdom and expertise in the difficult and urgent task of building a society that respects all its members in their dignity, their rights and their freedoms. This requires an attitude of reconciliation and calls for the Government and citizens of this land to be firmly committed to giving the best of themselves for the good of all. The challenge before you is great, but greater still are your capacity and determination to meet it.
The life and witness of Father Tansi remind us of the Gospel saying: "Blessed are the peacemakers" (Mt 5:9). Blessed are all who, in Nigeria and elsewhere in Africa, work for genuine peace. Blessed in the eyes of God are those working to lead the continent of Africa to a new phase of stability, reconciliation, development and progress.
Ultimate success in this venture will come from the Almighty, the Lord of life and of human history. Certain that he will sustain you in the work now before you, I make my own the words of the Psalmist: "May the Lord give strength to his people! May the Lord bless his people with peace!" (Ps 29:11).
As I begin my Visit, I express my deep esteem and affection for every Nigerian. I would willingly meet you all! May God be close to every son and daughter of this beloved land. God bless Nigeria!

*A villager from the town of Onitsha gives Pope John Paul II a gift during a mass which was celebrated in Onitsha March 22, 1998. Some two million pilgrims travelled from all over Nigeria to attend the mass and beutification ceremony for local Nigerian Father Cyprian Tansi.*

*Pope John Paul II waves to the crowd March 23, 1998 before the start of a mass in the village of Kubwa on the outskirts of the capital Abuja. This was the final public appearance of the Pope on his three day tour of Nigeria during which urged Nigeria's leader General Sani Abacha to make improvements in the human rights situation.*

*Pope John Paul II is greeted by children as he enters Rome's Piazza San Giovanni to address more than 20,000 young people from acroos Italy April 2, 1998. The Pope lamented a culture promising success and self-assertion at any cost, sex without responsibility and a lack of respect for others.*

*Pope John Paul II blesses the faithful gathered in St. Peter's Square for the Easter mass and his Urbi et Orbi (to the city and the World) message April 12, 1998.*

## URBI ET ORBI MESSAGE OF HIS HOLINESS POPE JOHN PAUL II

### EASTER SUNDAY 1998

1. "You know what took place regarding Jesus of Nazareth. . .we are witnesses to all that he did both in the country of the Jews and in Jerusalem" (cf. Acts 10:37-38).
These are the words which the Apostle Peter, a witness to the Resurrection of Christ, addressed to the centurion Cornelius and his household.
Today the witnesses speak: the eye-witnesses present at the events of Good Friday, those who were afraid before the Sanhedrin, those who on the third day found the tomb empty.
Witnesses to the Resurrection were, first, the women of Jerusalem and Mary of Magdala; and later the Apostles, informed by the women: first Peter and John, then all the rest.
Another witness was Saul of Tarsus, converted at the gates of Damascus, whom Christ permitted to experience the power of his resurrection, that he might become the chosen vessel of the missionary thrust of the early Church.

2. Yes, today the witnesses speak out: not only the first ones, the eye-witnesses, but also those who, from them, have learned the Easter message and have borne testimony to Christ crucified and risen from generation to generation.
Some have been witnesses even to the shedding of their blood and, thanks to them, the Church has continued on her way, also amid harsh persecutions and obstinate rejection.
On the strength of this unending testimony the Church has grown, and is now spread throughout the world.

Today is the feast of all witnesses; including those of our own century, who have proclaimed Christ in the midst of the "great tribulation" (Rev 7:14), confessing his death and resurrection in the concentration camps and the gulags, under the threat of bombs and guns, amid the terror unleashed by the blind hatred which has tragically engulfed individuals and whole nations.
Today they come from the great tribulation and sing the glory of Christ: in him, rising from the shadows of death, life has been made manifest.

3. Today, we too are witnesses to the Risen Christ and we repeat his proclamation of peace to all humanity on its way to the Third Millennium.
We bear witness to his death and resurrection, especially to the men and women of our own time, caught up in fratricidal strife and slaughter which reopen the wounds of ethnic rivalries, and, in different parts of every continent, especially in Africa and in Europe, are now sowing in the earth the seed of death and new conflicts for a sad tomorrow.
This proclamation of peace is for all those who are undergoing a calvary seemingly without end, thwarted in their aspiration for respect for their dignity and human rights, for justice, for employment, for fairer living conditions.
May this proclamation be an inspiration to the leaders of the nations and to every person of good will, especially in the Middle East and particularly in Jerusalem, where peace is put at risk by dangerous political decisions.
May it give fresh courage to those who have believed and still believe in dialogue as the way to settle national and international tensions.
May it fill everyone's heart with the boldness of the hope which springs from the truth being recognized and respected, so that new and promising prospects of solidarity may open up in the world.

4. Christ, who died and rose for us, you are the foundation of our hope!
We wish to make our own the testimony of Peter and that of countless other brothers and sisters down the centuries, in order to proclaim it again at the threshold of the new Millennium.
It is true: "The stone which the builders rejected has become the head of the corner" (Ps 118:22).
On this foundation is built the Church of the Living God, the Church of the Risen Christ.
In today's liturgy this Church sings a song both old and ever new.
With words filled with ardor she proclaims the victory of life over death:
"Mors et Vita duello conflixere mirando . . ."
"Death and life joined in a wondrous duel.
The Lord of life was dead; but now, alive, he triumphs".
And as though it had happened only yesterday, the Church turns to Mary of Magdala, who was the first to meet the Risen Lord:
"Dic nobis, Maria, quid vidisti in via?"
"Tell us, Mary, what did you see on the way?
The tomb of the living Christ, the glory of the Risen Christ, and his witnesses the angels, the shroud and his garments.
Christ, my hope, is risen; he goes before you into Galilee".

5. Today, you, the Risen One, wish to meet us in every corner of the earth, just as yesterday you met the Apostles in Galilee.
By virtue of this encounter we too can repeat:
"Scimus Christum surrexisse a mortuis vere:
tu nobis, victor Rex, miserere".
"Yes, we are certain: Christ is truly risen. Oh victorious King, bring us your salvation".

*Pope John Paul II passes two Swiss Guards as he takes his place for the weekly general audience in St. Peter's Square May 6, 1998. The Pope thanked the murdered Swiss Guard chief who shielded him in a 1981 assassination attempt and said the guardsman who killed the commandant and his wife would face God's judgement, referring to the triple killing, which took place May 4 of Swiss Guard commandant Alois Estermann, his wife Gladys Meza Romero, and vice corporal Cedric Tornay. The Vatican has said Tornay shot the Estermann's in their apartment in a moment of madness before shooting himself.*

*Queen Fabiola of Belgium sits behind bishops as she attends a beatification service in St. Peter's Square May 10, 1998. Twelve people were beatified by the Pope, including some 10 Spanish nuns, one of which was a distant relative of Queen Fabiola.*

*Pope John Paul II is greeted by pilgrims and citizens of Vercelli as he arrives in this northern city May 23, 1998. The Pope is in Vercelli to participate in celebrations for the 1,650th anniversary of the archdiocese and to beatify the priest Don Secondo Pollo.*

*South African President Nelson Mandela (L) talks with Pope John Paul II during their meeting at the Vatican June 18, 1998. Mandela thanked the Pope for the Catholic Church's help in education and health care of black South Africans when the white minority government wrote them off as second-class citizens.*

Some 40,000 people gather at Vienna's Heldenplatz square in front of the historic Hofburg palace for an open air mass celebrated by Pope John Paul II June 21, 1998. The three-day visit to Salzburg, St. Poelten and Vienna is the third by the 78-year-old pontiff to Austria and the 83rd foreign trip in his 20-year reign.

**Right:** Pope John Paul II greets the faithful as he arrives in the city of Chiavari at the start of a three-day trip to northern Italy September 18, 1998. The Pope will hold a mass and beatify Italian Giuseppe Antonio Tovini.

*Pope John Paul II rides in his popemobile as he arrives in Split harbour for an outdoor mass October 4, 1998. The Pope is on the last day of a three-day official visit to Croatia where he beatified World War Two-era Cardinal Alojzije Stepinac in a controversial tribute to a man hailed as a saint by Croats but condemned as a Nazi collaborator by communists.*

*Pope John Paul II leads a canonization ceremony in Rome October 11, 1998, of Edith Stein, a nun who converted to Christianity from the Jewish faith and died in Auschwitz during World War Two. Stein, born in 1891 into a Jewish family in what is now the Polish city of Wroclaw, was deported to Auschwitz concentration camp in August 1942 by the Nazis and met her death in the gas chambers later that month.*

Pope John Paul II is cheered by pilgrims and faithful as he arrives with the popemobile in St Peter's Square October 16, 1998. An emotional Pope marked the 20th anniversary of his election on Friday asking his Polish countrymen to pray so that he could fulfill his dream of leading the Catholic Church into the next millennium.

*Left: Pope John Paul II greets pilgrims gathered in St. Peter's Square prior to his weekly audience November 11, 1998. The pope greeted his fellow Polish countrymen at the audience by making a reference to the 80th anniversary of the independence of Poland.*

*Men from the Pacific Islands dressed in traditional costumes walk towards Pope John Paul II during a ceremony in St. Peter's Basilica to inaugurate a special assembly of bishops from Oceania November 22, 1998. The bishops synod will end on December 12 with another ceremony in the Basilica.*

*Pope John Paul II (top) presides over the first day of the assembly for the bishops of Oceania at the Vatican November 23, 1998. The synod was opened officially on November 23 with a solemn ceremony in St. Peter's Basilica.*

## URBI ET ORBI MESSAGE OF HIS HOLINESS
## POPE JOHN PAUL II

### Christmas 1998

1. *"Regem venturum Dominum, venite, adoremus".*
*"Come, let us adore the King, the Lord, who is to come".*
How many times have we repeated these words throughout the season of Advent, echoing the expectation of all humanity.
Straining towards the future from his very origins, man thirsts for God, the fullness of life.
From the beginning he has invoked a Saviour to free him from evil and death, to fulfil his need for happiness.
In the Garden of Eden, after the first sin, God the Father, faithful and merciful, had foretold to him the coming of a Saviour (cf. Gn 3:15), who would restore the broken covenant, and create a new relationship of friendship, understanding and peace.

*Pope John Paul II blesses pilgrims from the central balcony of the St. Peter's facade during his Urbi Et Orbi (to the city and the world) Christmas message December 25, 1998. The Pope called for a ban on the death penalty around the world and said that senseless violence and abuse of human dignity had blurred the joy of the Christmas season for many people.*

2. This joyful message, entrusted to the children of Abraham, from the time of the Exodus from Egypt (cf. Ex 3:6-8), has echoed down the centuries as a cry of hope on the lips of Israel's Prophets, who time and again reminded the people:
*"Prope est Dominus: venite, adoremus!"*
*"The Lord is near; come let us adore him!".*
Come to adore the God who does not forsake those who seek him with a sincere heart and strive to keep his law.
Heed his message which strengthens hearts broken and confused.
*Prope est Dominus:* faithful to his ancient promise, God the Father has now brought it to pass in the mystery of Christmas.

3. Yes, his promise, which nourished the trusting expectation of countless believers, has become a gift in Bethlehem, in the heart of the Holy Night. Yesterday the Liturgy of the Mass reminded us of it:
*"Hodie scietis quia veniet Dominus, et mane videbitis gloriam eius".*
*"Today you will know that the Lord comes: at daybreak you will see his glory".*
Last night we saw the glory of God, proclaimed by the joyful singing of the angels; we have adored the King, the Lord of the universe, together with the shepherds keeping watch over their flock.
With the eyes of faith we too have seen, placed in a manger, the Messiah, the Prince of Peace, and beside him the Virgin Mother in silent adoration.

4. Today we join the angelic host, the enraptured shepherds; we too sing in exultation:
*"Christus natus est nobis: venite, adoremus".*
*"Christ is born for us: come, let us adore him".*
From the night of Bethlehem until today, the Birth of the Lord continues to inspire hymns of joy which express the tenderness of God, sown in the hearts of men.
In all the world's tongues, the event most grand and most lowly is being celebrated: Emmanuel, God with us for ever.
How many expressive songs has Christmas inspired in every people and culture!
Who has not known the emotions they express?
Their melodies bring alive once more the mystery of the Holy Night; they tell of the encounter between the Gospel and the paths of mankind.
Yes, Christmas has entered the hearts of the peoples, who look to Bethlehem with shared wonderment.
The General Assembly of the United Nations has also, unanimously, recognized the little city of Judah (cf. Mt 2:6) as the land where the celebration of Jesus's birth will be, in the year 2000, a unique occasion for projects of hope and peace.

5. How can we fail to notice the strident contrast between the serenity of the Christmas carols and the many problems of the present hour?
We know the disturbing developments from the reports coming each day from television and the newspapers, sweeping from one hemisphere to the other of the globe: tragic situations, which often involve human guilt and even malice, soaked in fratricidal hate and senseless violence.
May the light coming from Bethlehem save us from the danger of becoming resigned to so tormented and distressing a scenario.
May the proclamation of Christmas be a source of encouragement to all those who work to bring relief to the tormented situation in the Middle East by respecting international commitments.
May Christmas help to strengthen and renew, throughout the world, the consensus concerning the need for urgent and adequate measures to halt the production and sale of arms, to defend human life, to end the death penalty, to free children and adolescents from all forms of exploitation, to restrain the bloodied hand of those responsible for genocide and crimes of war, to give environmental issues, especially after the recent natural catastrophes, the indispensable attention which they deserve for the protection of creation and of human dignity!

6. May the joy of Christmas, which sings of the birth of the Saviour, instil in all trust in the power of truth and of patient perseverance in doing good.
For each of us the divine message of Bethlehem resounds:
*"Be not afraid; for behold, I bring you good news of a great joy, to you is born this day in the city of David a Saviour, who is Christ the Lord"* (Lk 2:10-11).
Today there shines forth, *Urbi et Orbi,* upon the city of Rome and upon the whole world, the face of God: Jesus reveals him to us as the Father who loves us.
All you who are seeking the meaning of life, all you whose hearts are burning with the hope of salvation, freedom and peace, come to meet the Child born of Mary:
He is God, our Saviour, the only one worthy of this name, the one Lord.

*He is born for us, come, let us adore him!*

*Pope John Paul II waves to the faithful gathered in St. Peter's Basilica at the end of a solemn ceremony for the Roman Catholic Churches World Day of Peace January 1, 1999. The Pope recalled the atrocities of the 20th century but also hailed an age that enshrined respect for human rights as a universal duty.*

*Pope John Paul II lays his hands on the head of new Irish bishop Diarmuid Martin during a consecration ceremony in St. Peter's Basilica January 6, 1999. The Pope traditionally consecrates new bishops during a mass on the feast of the Epiphany, the day the Church commemorates the visit of the Magi to the infant Jesus.*

*Pope John Paul II baptises Genevieve Maude Marie de Meeus d'Argentueil of Switzerland, as her parents look on during a baptism ceremony in Michelangelo's Sistine Chapel at the Vatican January 10, 1999. The Pope baptised 19 newborn babies in a ceremony to mark the Roman Catholic feast of the baptism of Jesus.*

*An unidentified child with a baby bottle in his hands approaches Pope John Paul II at the end of a baptism ceremony in the Michelangelo's Sistine Chapel at the Vatican January 10, 1999.*

Pope John Paul II greets teenage singing prodigy Charlotte Church at the Vatican in this January 13, 1999 file photo.

**Left:** Pope John Paul II waves to over 100,000 worshippers attending his last public event as he arrives by Popemobile to Mexico City's Azteca stadium January 25, 1999. Pope John Paul II is holding a 'meeting with the generations' at the famous Mexico City stadium which will be linked up with five other cities in the Americas from Los Angeles to Buenos Aires.

*Pope John Paul II waves at the faithful, flanked by Cardinal Norberto Rivera, primate of the Catholic Church in Mexico, after arriving at the Azteca stadium where an estimated 110,000 people are present to witness the Pope's last public event in Mexico January 25, 1999.*

*Pope John Paul II delivers his speech under a huge cross at the 'Light of the World' papal youth gathering January 26, 1999. Thousands of youths from all over the U.S. bused to the site for the rally on the first day of the Pope's two-day visit. The 78-year-old Pontiff arrived in St. Louis following a five-day visit to Mexico.*

## ADDRESS OF JOHN PAUL II

## TO THE YOUNG PEOPLE AT THE KIEL CENTER

St. Louis, January 26, 1999

Part I

*Dear Young People of St. Louis,*
*Dear Young People of the United States,*
*Praised be Jesus Christ!*

*1. Your warm and enthusiastic welcome makes me very happy. It tells me that tonight the Pope belongs to you. I have just been in Mexico City, to celebrate the conclusion of the Synod of Bishops for America. There I had the joy of being with many thousands of young people. And now, my joy continues here with you, the young people of St. Louis and Missouri, and of the whole United States.*

*2. We are gathered here this evening to listen to Jesus as he speaks to us through his word and in the power of the Holy Spirit.*
*We have just heard the Apostle Paul say to Timothy, his young fellow evangelizer: "Train yourself for devotion" (1 Tim 4:7). These are important words for every Christian, for everyone who truly seeks to follow the Lord and to put his words into practice. They are especially important for you, the young people of the Church. And so you need to ask yourselves: what training am I doing in order to live a truly Christian life?*
*You all know what "training" is, and what it signifies. In fact, we are here in the Kiel Center where many people train long and hard in order to compete in different sports. Today, this impressive stadium has become another kind of training ground — not for hockey or soccer or basketball, but for that training that will help you to live your faith in Jesus more decisively. This is the "training in devotion" that Saint Paul is referring to — the training that makes it possible for you to give yourselves without reservation to the Lord and to the work that he calls you to do!*

*3. I am told that there was much excitement in St. Louis during the recent baseball season, when two great players (Mark McGwire and Sammy Sosa) were competing to break the home-run record. You can feel the same great enthusiasm as you train for a different goal: the goal of following Christ, the goal of bringing his message to the world. Each one of you belongs to Christ, and Christ belongs to you. At Baptism you were claimed for Christ with the Sign of the Cross; you received the Catholic faith as a treasure to be shared with others. In Confirmation, you were sealed with the gifts of the Holy Spirit and strengthened for your Christian mission and vocation. In the Eucharist, you receive the food that nourishes you for the spiritual challenges of each day.*
*I am especially pleased that so many of you had the opportunity today to receive the Sacrament of Penance, the Sacrament of Reconciliation. In this Sacrament you experience the Savior's tender mercy and love in a most personal way, when you are freed from sin and from its ugly companion which is shame. Your burdens are lifted and you experience the joy of new life in Christ.*
*Your belonging to the Church can find no greater expression or support than by sharing in the Eucharist every Sunday in your parishes. Christ gives us the gift of his body and blood to make us one body, one spirit in him, to bring us more deeply into communion with him and with all the members of his Body, the Church. Make the Sunday celebration in your parishes a real encounter with Jesus in the community of his followers: this is an essential part of your "training in devotion" to the Lord!*

*4. Dear young friends, in the Reading we have just heard, the Apostle Paul tells Timothy: "Let no one have contempt for your youth" (1 Tim 4:12). He says this because youth is a marvelous gift of God. It is a time of special energies, special opportunities and special responsibilities. Christ and the Church need your special talents. Use well the gifts the Lord has given you!*
*This is the time of your "training", of your physical, intellectual, emotional and spiritual development. But this does not mean that you can put off until later your meeting with Christ and your sharing in the Church's mission. Even though you are young, the time for action is now! Jesus does not have "contempt for your youth". He does not set you aside for a later time when you will be older and your training will be complete. Your training will never be finished. Christians are always in training. You are ready for what Christ wants of you now. He wants you — all of you — to be light to the world, as only young people can be light. It is time to let your light shine!*
*In all my travels I tell the world about your youthful energies, your gifts and your readiness to love and serve. And wherever I go I challenge young people — as a friend — to live in the light and truth of Jesus Christ.*
*I urge you to let his word enter your hearts, and then from the bottom of your hearts to tell him: "Here I am Lord, I come to do your will!" (cf. Heb 10:7).*

Part II

*"You are the light of the world. . . Your light must shine before all" (Mt 5:14.16).*
*Dear Young People,*

*1. Ask yourselves: Do I believe these words of Jesus in the Gospel? Jesus is calling you the light of the world. He is asking you to let your light shine before others. I know that in your hearts you want to say: "Here I am, Lord. Here I am. I come to do your will" (Responsorial Psalm; cf. Heb 10:7). But only if you are one with Jesus can you share his light and be a light to the world.*
*Are you ready for this?*
*Sadly, too many people today are living apart from the light — in a world of illusions, a world of fleeting shadows and promises unfulfilled. If you look to Jesus, if you live the Truth that is Jesus, you will have in you the light that reveals the truths and values on which to build your own happiness, while building a world of justice, peace and solidarity. Remember what Jesus said: "I am the light of the world; those who follow me will not walk in darkness, but will have the light of life" (cf. Jn 8:12).*
*Because Jesus is the Light, we too become light when we proclaim him. This is the heart of the Christian mission to which each of you has been called through Baptism and Confirmation. You are called to make the light of Christ shine brightly in the world.*

*2. When you were little, were you sometimes afraid of the dark? Today you are no longer children afraid of the dark. You are teenagers and young adults. But already you realize that there is another kind of darkness in the world: the darkness of doubt and uncertainty. You may feel the darkness of loneliness and isolation. Your anxieties may come from questions about your future, or regrets about past choices.*
*Sometimes the world itself seems filled with darkness. The darkness of children who go hungry and even die. The darkness of homeless people who lack work and proper medical care. The darkness of violence: violence against the unborn child, violence in families, the violence of gangs, the violence of sexual abuse, the violence of drugs that destroy the body, mind and heart. There is something terribly wrong when so many young people are overcome by hopelessness to the point of taking their own lives. And already in parts of this nation, laws have been passed which allow doctors to end the lives of the very people they are sworn to help. God's gift of life is being rejected. Death is chosen over life, and this brings with it the darkness of despair.*

*3. But you believe in the light (cf. Jn 12:36)! Do not listen to those who encourage you to lie, to shirk responsibility, to put yourselves first. Do not listen to those who tell you that chastity is passé. In your hearts you know that true love is a gift from God and respects his plan for the union of man and woman in marriage. Do not be taken in by false values and deceptive slogans, especially about your freedom. True freedom is a wonderful gift from God, and it has been a cherished part of your country's history. But when freedom is separated from truth, individuals lose their moral direction and the very fabric of society begins to unravel.*
*Freedom is not the ability to do anything we want, whenever we want. Rather, freedom is the ability to live responsibly the truth of our relationship with God and with one another. Remember what Jesus said: "you will know the truth and the truth will set you free" (Jn 8:32). Let no one mislead you or prevent you from seeing what really matters. Turn to Jesus, listen to him, and discover the true meaning and direction of your lives.*

*4. You are children of the light (cf. Jn 12:36)! You belong to Christ, and he has called you by name. Your first responsibility is to get to know as much as you can about him, in your parishes, in religious instruction in your high schools and colleges, in your youth groups and Newman Centers.*
*But you will get to know him truly and personally only through prayer. What is needed is that you talk to him, and listen to him.*
*Today we are living in an age of instant communications. But do you realize what a unique form of communication prayer is? Prayer enables us to meet God at the most profound level of our being. It connects us directly to God: Father, Son and Holy Spirit, in a constant exchange of love.*
*Through prayer you will learn to become the light of the world, because in prayer you become one with the source of our true light, Jesus himself.*

*5. Each of you has a special mission in life, and you are each called to be a disciple of Christ. Many of you will serve God in the vocation of Christian married life; some of you will serve him as dedicated single persons; some as priests and religious. But all of you must be the light of the world. To those of you who think that Christ may be inviting you to follow him in the priesthood or the consecrated life I make this personal appeal: I ask you to open your hearts generously to him; do not delay your response. The Lord will help you to know his will; he will help you to follow your vocation courageously.*

6. Young friends, in the days and weeks and years ahead, for as long as you remember this evening, remember that the Pope came to the United States, to the City of St. Louis, to call the young people of America to Christ, to invite you to follow him. He came to challenge you to be the light of the world! "The light shines in the darkness and the darkness does not overcome it" (Jn 1:5). Jesus who has conquered sin and death reminds you: "I am with you always" (Mt 28:20). He says: "Courage! It is I; have no fear" (Mk 6:50).

On the horizon of this city stands the Gateway Arch, which often catches the sunlight in its different colors and hues. In a similar way, in a thousand different ways, you must reflect the light of Christ through your lives of prayer and joyful service of others. With the help of Mary, the Mother of Jesus, the young people of America will do this magnificently!

Remember: Christ is calling you; the Church needs you; the Pope believes in you and he expects great things of you!

Praised be Jesus Christ!

At the end of the service some of the young people gave the Holy Father a hockey stick and jersey. The Pope appreciated the gift and said extemporaneously:

So, I am prepared to return once more to play hockey! But if I will be able to, that is the question. Perhaps after this meeting I will be a bit more ready!

**Pope John Paul II waves to the crowd as President Clinton applauds after arriving in St. Louis January 26, 1999. Pope John Paul II is on a two-day visit to the United States.**

**Pope John Paul II drinks from an historic chalice during his mass at the Trans World Dome January 27, 1999. The gold chalice was used in the first mass celebrated 300 years ago in the wilderness that became present-day St. Louis. The chalice was brought to the French colonial frontier from Quebec in 1698 by the Rev. Jean St. Cosme, a Canadian-born priest ordained in 1690.**

*Pope John Paul II receives a hug from a child during the presentation of gifts while celebrating mass at the TWA Dome January 27, 1999. The Pope celebrated mass before 100,000 people in the domed stadium.*

*Pope John Paul II walks amongst children as he arrives to celebrate mass in Rome's parish church of San Fulgenzio February 14, 1999. The Pope usually visits a parish church when he does not have an official ceremony at the Vatican.*

*A child looks at Pope John Paul II as the 78-year-old Pontiff arrives for a visit to Rome's parish church of St. Raimondo Nonnato February 21, 1999.*

**Left:** *Pope John Paul II sits beneath an image of French priest Nicolas Barre, one of ten people who were beatified, or put on the road to sainthood in the Roman Catholic Church, during the ceremony March 7, 1999. Others who were beatified included eight people killed in the 1936-39 Spanish Civil War, and German Anna Schaffer who spread the apostolic faith despite a life of paralysis and disease before dying in 1925.*

*Above:* President Mohammad Khatami (L) talks with Pope John Paul II during their meeting at the Vatican March 11, 1999. Khatami takes his revolution of openness to the Vatican, stepping from one divinely inspired state to another as he holds a historic meeting with Pope John Paul.

*Left:* Pope John Paul II (L) looks at a copy of the new 'Abba Pater' CD as he meets the General Director of Radio Vatican father Borgomeo at the end of the Pontiff's weekly general audience at Vatican March 17, 1999. Sony and Vatican Radio release today the Abba Pater CD of religious music featuring reflections by Pope John Paul II.

*Right Top:* Rome's ancient Colosseum is packed with people during the traditional candlelit Via Crucis (Way of the Cross) procession held by Pope John Paul II April 2, 1999. The Via Crucis Way of the Cross is part of the Good Friday ceremonies.

*Right Bottom:* Pope John Paul II smiles as he receives flowers from two children during the Pontiff's visit to the Rome's University of Tor Vergata April 29, 1999. Pope John Paul has written to U.N. Secretary-General Kofi Annan praising his bid for peace in the Balkans and urging an end to the cycle of hatred and violence, the Vatican said on Thursday.

*Pope John Paul II walks with Romanian Orthodox Patriarch Teoctist in to the altar, during a orthodox mass in Bucharest Palace May 9, 1999. Pope John Paul ll is on a historic trip to Romania, the first by a Pontiff to a mainly Orthodox country, by paying tribute to Christians who paid with their blood during the 'winter of communism'.*

German Chancellor Gerhard Schroeder gestures as he poses with Pope John Paul II in the Vatican May 18, 1999. The Pontiff, who turned 79 on Tuesday, and Schroeder discussed the conflict in the Balkans and the need for a just and honourable solution to the crisis.

**Right:** Pope John Paul II greets U.N. Secretary General Kofi Annan after he arrived at the Vatican to hold talks on the Kosovo conflict June 3, 1999. The Pope told Annan that the United Nations should oversee an end of hostilities in Yugoslavia and the return of refugees to Kosovo.

*Pope John Paul II prays at a Corpus Domini mass which was dedicated to peace in the Balkans June 3, 1999. The Pope said that the breakthrough in the Yugoslav crisis was a comforting ray of hope for the region. The 79-year-old Pope held talks on the Kosovo crisis earlier in the day with U.N. Secretary-General Kofi Annan.*

*Polish-born Pope John Paul II (L) shakes hands with a boy and a girl before his departure from the town of Lichen June 7, 1999. The 79-year-old Pontiff is in his native country for a 13-day trip that will take him back to his roots and redouble the faith of millions of his largely Roman Catholic country folks.*

*Pope John Paul II waves to pilgrims as he arrives to celebrate the Holy Mass in Siedlce June 10, 1999. The 79 year-old Pontiff is on a 13-day visit to his native Poland.*

*Polish President wife Jolanta Kwasnieska kisses the hand of Pope John Paul II during the welcoming ceremony in front of Presidential Palace in Warsaw, June 11, 1999, as Polish President (L) looks on. The 79-year-old Polish-born Pontiff is in Warsaw during his 13-day trip where he addressed both houses of the parliament. It's the first time that the Pope has addressed any national parliaments.*

*Pope John Paul II smiles as he jokes with the pilgrims as he adresses the crowd in front of the basilica in Wadowice June 16, 1999. The 79-year-old Pontiff continues his 13-days visit to his home country Poland with a visit to Wadowice where he was born in 1920.*

## JOHN PAUL II
## Homily

Wednesday, 16 June 1999, Wadowice

*1. Once again, during my service to the universal Church in the See of Saint Peter, I come to my native town of Wadowice. With great emotion I gaze upon this city of my childhood years, which witnessed my first steps, my first words and those "first bows" which, as Norwid puts it, are "like the eternal profession of Christ: 'Be praised!'" (cf. Moja piosenka [My Song]). The city of my childhood, my family home, the church of my Baptism . . . I wish to cross these hospitable thresholds, bow before my native soil and its inhabitants, and utter the words of greeting given to family members upon on their return from a long journey: "Praised be Jesus Christ!"*

*With these words I greet all the people of Wadowice, from the elderly, to whom I am linked by the bonds of childhood and adolescence, to the children, who are seeing for the first time the Pope who has come to visit them. I greet the beloved Cardinal Franciszek and thank him because, as Pastor of the Archdiocese, he has shown constant concern for my native town. I greet the Auxiliary Bishops and the retired Bishops. I thank the visiting Bishops who are accompanying me along this pilgrimage. I extend heartfelt greetings to the priests, especially those from both Prefectures of Wadowice, and among them the parish priest of this parish. I entrust to God the late Father Tadeusz Zacher and all the deceased priests who exercised their pastoral ministry in this city. I warmly embrace all the families of Religious who serve in the Wadowice area.*

*In a particular way I wish to greet the Discalced Carmelite Fathers of Górka in Wadowice. We are meeting on an exceptional occasion: 27 August this year marks the centenary of the consecration of the Church of Saint Joseph, at the Convent founded by Saint Raphael Kalinowski. As I did as a young man, I now return in spirit to that place of particular devotion to Our Lady of Mount Carmel, which had such a great influence on the spirituality of the Wadowice area. I myself received many graces there, and today I wish to thank the Lord for them. I am pleased that I was able to beatify, together with one hundred and eight martyrs, Blessed Father Alfons Maria Mazurek, a pupil and later a worthy teacher in the minor seminary attached to the Convent. I had the opportunity to meet personally this witness of Christ who in 1944, as prior of the convent of Czerna, confirmed his fidelity to God by a martyr's death. I kneel in veneration before his relics, which rest in the Church of Saint Joseph, and I give thanks to God for the gift of the life, martyrdom and holiness of this great Religious.*

*2. Jerusalem, "for love of the house of the Lord, I will ask for your good" (Ps 122:9). Today I make my own these words of the Psalmist and I apply them to this town. Wadowice, town of my childhood, for love of the house — my family home and the house of the Lord — I will ask for your good! How can I not make this promise, as Providence has enabled me today to be present here, on a bridge as it were, which connects these two houses — my family home and the house of God? It is an extraordinary, and yet most natural, coming together of two places which — like no others — leave a deep mark on the heart.*

*With filial affection, I embrace the threshold of the home of my birth, giving thanks to divine Providence for the gift of life passed on to me by my beloved parents, for the warmth of the family home, for the love of my dear ones, who gave me a sense of security and strength, even when they had to face death and the difficulties of daily life in troubled times.*

*With profound veneration I also embrace the threshold of the house of God, the parish church of Wadowice, and in it the Baptistery, in which I was joined to Christ and received into the community of his Church. In this church I made my first Confession and received my First Holy Communion. Here I was an altar boy. Here I gave thanks to God for the gift of the priesthood and, as Archbishop of Kraków, I celebrated the Twenty-fifth Anniversary of my Ordination to the Priesthood. God alone, the giver of every grace, knows what goodness and what manifold graces I received from this church and from this parish community. To him, the Triune God, I give glory today at the doors of this church.*

*Finally, with childlike trust, I turn to the Chapel of the Holy Cross, to gaze again upon the image of Our Lady of Perpetual Help in Wadowice. I do it with even greater joy, because today I crown this image, as a sign of our love for the Mother of the Saviour and for her divine Son. This sign is all the more expressive because I am told that these crowns were made with your gifts, often very precious, and associated with many special memories, people's lives, their difficulties, or the noble sentiments of families, spouses and engaged couples. To this material gift you have added the great gift of the spirit — the prayer of entrustment to the Mother of Christ who has visited your homes. I am sure that your ardent love for Mary will never be without a response. This mutual bond of love is itself, in a sense, a source of grace and a pledge of the unfailing help which through Mary's intercession we receive from her divine Son.*

*3. "When the time had fully come, God sent forth his Son, born of woman" (Gal 4:4). These words of Saint Paul, which we have heard today, bring us in a certain sense to the very heart of this mystery. The fullness of time came with the mystery of the Incarnation of the Eternal Word. The Son of God came into the world to accomplish the Father's saving plan, to bring about the redemption of man and restore him to the sonship which he had lost. In this mystery Mary has a special place. God called her to become the woman by whom the original sin of the first woman would be undone. God needed this mediation of Mary. He needed her free consent, her obedience and her devotion, in order to reveal fully his eternal love for humanity.*

*The Apostle of the Nations would later write: "Because you are sons, God has sent the Spirit of his Son into our hearts, crying: 'Abba, Father!'" (Gal 4:6). We also know that this event took place in the presence of Mary. Just as she was present at the beginning of Christ's work of redemption, so too, on the day of Pentecost, she was present at the beginning of the Church. She, who on the day of the Annunciation was filled with the Holy Spirit, was the special witness of the Spirit's presence on the day of Pentecost. She who owed her own motherhood to the mysterious working of the Spirit was able, more than anyone else, to understand the significance of the descent of the Consoler. Mary, as no other, recognized the moment in which the life of the Church began — the life of that community of men and women who are made members of Christ and can call upon God as Father. No one in the world has been given an experience of the Trinitarian love of the Father, the Son and the Holy Spirit to the same extent as Mary, the Mother of the Word Incarnate.*

*And so, as we prepare to celebrate the Great Jubilee of the Redemption, we turn in a special way to her as a unique guide on the paths of salvation. If the Jubilee is meant to make us aware of all that was accomplished by the Incarnation of the Son of God, we cannot fail to imitate the experience of the faith, hope and love of the Mother of Christ. We cannot fail to turn to her. From Mary, in fact, we learn the openness to the Spirit which enables us to enjoy more fully the fruits of Christ's Death and Resurrection. The conviction that the Mother of God has a unique role in the life of the Church and of every Christian was always dear to our forefathers. Over the last hundred years the people of Wadowice expressed this in a special way when they gathered to venerate the image of Our Lady of Perpetual Help and made her the Patron of their personal, family and social life. In 1935 Father Leonard Prochownik, a local priest, wrote: "Our Lady of Perpetual Help is venerated here. She has her chapel, where her miraculous image is placed, and there many people have personally experienced and continue to experience how much she shows her goodness and hastens to assist them in their temporal and spiritual needs". And that was true; I can personally testify to this. And I believe that it is still true today. May it also be true in the future!*

*4. During my first visit to Wadowice, I asked you to surround me with constant prayer before the image of this Mother. I see that my request has been inscribed in stone. I believe this is a sign that my request has also remained deeply engraved in your hearts. Today, I thank you warmly today for this prayer. I always feel it at work and I ask you to continue to pray for me. I have so much need of your prayer. The Church has so much need of it. The entire world has need of it.*

*There is one other thing for which I want to thank you. I know that in Wadowice the Church of Kraków, together with its Archbishop, has built a particular votive shrine of our thanksgiving to the Mother of God. Not far from here a Home for Single Mothers has been built. Those women who, despite the difficulties and sacrifices, wish to keep the fruit of their motherhood can find shelter and help there. I am grateful for this great gift of your love for the human person and your concern for life. I am all the more grateful because the Home is named after my mother Emilia. I believe that she who brought me into the world and filled my childhood with love will also watch over this undertaking. I ask you to continue to support this house with your goodness.*

*5. Sub tuum praesidium . . .*
*We fly to your protection, O Mary.*
*To your protection we entrust the history of this town, of the Church of Kraków and the whole country.*
*To your maternal love we entrust the lives of each individual, of our families and of society as a whole.*
*Despise not our petitions in our need, but deliver us always from every danger.*
*Mary, obtain for us the grace of faith, hope and love, so that following your example and guidance, we may carry into the new Millennium our witness to the Father's love, to the redeeming Death and Resurrection of the Son and to the sanctifying work of the Holy Spirit.*
*Be with us at all times!*
*O glorious and blessed Virgin,*
*Our Lady,*
*Our Advocate,*
*Our Mediatrix,*
*Our Consolatrix,*
*Our Mother! Amen.*

*Pope John Paul II kisses the gospel during the Holy Mass for St. Peter and Paul festivities in the Vatican June 29, 1999. The Pope said he had a strong yearning to visit Biblical sites in Iraq and Egypt, and Holy Land cities ruled by Israel and the Palestinian Authority as part of millennium celebrations.*

Pope John Paul II looking rested and tanned midway through a 20-day private mountain retreat holiday greets wellwishers July 18, 1999 at the chalet where he is staying in the Italian Alps val d'Aosta region near the French border. The Pope on Sunday prayed for John F. Kennedy Jr. when he heard of the plane crash presumed to have killed him and recalled a string of tragedies that have plagued America's first political family.

**Left:** Irish popstar Bono of supergroup U2 gives Pope John Paul II his sunglasses during a private audience September 23, 1999 with members of the Jubilee 2000 lobby group which is urging rich countries to write off the unpayable debts of the poorest countries by the new millennium. Bono said he told the pontiff that he was not only a 'great holy man' but also a 'great showman' and that the Pope even tried the shades on.

Pope John Paul II shakes hands with Shankaracharya Madhavananda Saraswati, a Hindu holy man at an inter-religious leaders meeting in New Delhi, November 7, 1999. The pope is scheduled to leave for Georgia tomorrow morning after concluding a four-day visit to India.

Pope John Paul II waves to followers at New Delhi's Jawaharlal Nehru Stadium November 7, 1999. Behind the pope, is a painting of the late Mother Theresa of Calcutta. The pontiff declared that Asia will be the evangelical focus of the Roman Catholic church in the next millennium.

*Pope John Paul II waves from the popemobile to the tens of thousands of faithful gathered at New Delhi's Jawaharlal Nehru Stadium November 7, 1999 to hear the holy mass. The pope delivered the mass on the last full day of his four-day visit to India.*

*Pope John Paul II (L) and the Patriarch of Georgia, Ilya II (R), sit in front of an Orthodox icon at the patriarch's residence in Tbilisi November 8, 1999 at the start of the pontiff's visit to Georgia. This was Pope John Paul II first visit to Georgia.*

Pope John Paul II (L) walks with Georgian President Eduard Shevardnadze (R) during their meeting in Tbilisi in November 9, 1999. The Pope arrived on his first visit to predominantly Orthodox Georgia on Monday.

Swedish King Carl Gustaf XVI stands next to Pope John Paul II as Queen Silvia looks on during a private audience at the Vatican November 13, 1999. The Swedish Royals are on a private visit to attend an ecumenical service where a statue of Sweden's St. Bridget, a 14th century Swedish noble woman, will be inaugurated November 13.

*Brazilian President Fernando Henrique Cardoso (L) poses with Pope John Paul II under a painting of the resurrection of Jesus Christ, during his private audience at the Vatican, November 19, 1999. President Cardoso and his wife are in Italy for an official six-day visit.*

*Pope John Paul II walks out accompanied by Cardinal Edmund Casimir Szoka (L) and Bishop Piero Marini (R) at the end of the ceremony to inaugurate the restored Sistine Chapel, December 11, 1999. The works involved the restoration of a dozen frescoes painted in the 1400's at the second level of the chapel during a two-decade project that cleaned some of the world's most precious frescoes in the room where Popes are elected.*

*Pope John Paul II looks at a Lancia car in the Vatican December 22, 1999. The 'Lancia Giubileo' car, which is a gift from Italian carmaker Fiat for Pope John Paul II, is derived from a prototype and is a unique model measuring five-metres and weighing around two-tons.*

## URBI ET ORBI

Christmas Day, 25 December 1999

1. "To us a child is born, to us a son is given" (Is 9:6).

Today the "good news" of Christmas rings out in the Church and in the world. It rings out in the words of the Prophet Isaiah, called the "evangelist" of the Old Testament, who speaks of the mystery of the redemption as if he saw the events of seven centuries later.
Words inspired by God, surprising words which come down through history, and today, on the threshold of the Year 2000, re-echo all through the earth, proclaiming the great mystery of the Incarnation.

2. "To us a child is born".
These prophetic words are fulfilled in the narrative of the Evangelist Luke, who describes the "event", full of ever new wonder and hope.
On that night in Bethlehem, Mary gave birth to a Child, whom she called Jesus.
There was no room for them in the Inn; and so the Mother gave birth to the Son in a stable, and laid him in a manger. The Evangelist John, in the Prologue of his Gospel, penetrates the "mystery" of this event.
The One born in the stable is the eternal Son of God.
He is the Word who was in the beginning, the Word who was with God, the Word who was God.
All things that were made were made through him (cf. Jn 1:1-3).
The eternal Word, the Son of God, took the nature of man.
God the Father "so loved the world that he gave his only Son" (Jn 3:16).
When the Prophet Isaiah says: "to us a child is born", he reveals, in all its fulness, the mystery of Christmas: the eternal generation of the Word of the Father, his birth in time through the work of the Holy Spirit.

3. The circle of the mystery widens:
the Evangelist John writes:
"The Word became flesh and dwelt among us" (Jn 1:14); and he adds: "to all who received him, who believed in his name, he gave power to become children of God" (1:12).
The circle of the mystery widens: the birth of the Son of God is the sublime gift, the greatest grace for man's benefit that the human mind could ever have imagined.
Remembering the birth of Christ on this holy Day, we live, together with this event, the "mystery of man's divine adoption" through the work of Christ who comes into the world.
For this reason, Christmas Night and Christmas Day are perceived as "sacred" by those who seek the truth. We Christians profess them to be "holy", because in them we recognize the unmistakable stamp of the One who is Holy, full of mercy and goodness.

4. This year there is yet another reason which makes more holy this day of grace: it is the beginning of the Great Jubilee. Last night, before Holy Mass, I opened the Holy Door of the Vatican Basilica. A symbolic act, which inaugurates the Jubilee Year, a gesture which highlights with singular eloquence something already present in the mystery of Christmas: Jesus, born of Mary in the poverty of Bethlehem, He, the Eternal Son given to us by the Father, is, for us and for everyone, the Door!
The Door of our salvation, the Door of life, the Door of peace!
This is the message of Christmas and the proclamation of the Great Jubilee.

5. We turn our gaze to you, o Christ, Door of our salvation, as we thank you for all the good of the years, centuries and millennia which have passed.
We must however confess that humanity has sometimes sought the Truth elsewhere, invented false certainties, and chased after deceptive ideologies.
At times people have refused to respect and love their brothers and sisters of a different race or faith; they have denied fundamental rights to individuals and nations.
But you continue to offer to all the splendour of the Truth which saves.
We look to you, O Christ, Door of Life, and we thank you for the wonders with which you have enriched every generation.
At times this world neither respects nor loves life.
But you never cease to love life; indeed, in the mystery of Christmas, you come to enlighten people's minds, so that legislators and political leaders, men and women of good will, may be committed to welcoming human life as a precious gift.
You come to give us the Gospel of Life. We lift our eyes to you, O Christ, Door of peace, as, pilgrims in time, we visit all the places of grief and of war, the resting places of the victims of brutal conflicts and cruel slaughter.
You, Prince of Peace, invite us to ban the senseless use of arms, and the recourse to violence and hatred which have doomed individuals, peoples and continents.

6. "To us a son is given".
You, Father, have given us your Son.
And you give him to us again today, at the dawn of the new millennium.
For us he is the Door. Through him we enter a new dimension and we reach the fulness of the destiny of salvation which you have prepared for all.
Precisely for this reason, Father, you gave us your Son, so that humanity would know what it is that you wish to give us in eternity, so that human beings would have the strength to fulfil your mysterious plan of love.
Christ, Son of the ever Virgin Mother, light and hope of those who seek you even when they do not know you, and of those who, knowing you, seek you all the more.
Christ, you are the Door!
Through you, in the power of the Holy Spirit, we wish to enter the third millennium.

You, O Christ, are the same yesterday, today and for ever (cf. Heb 13:8).

*Pope John Paul II holds the Holy Bible as he enters the Holy Door in St. Peter's Basilica December 24, 1999. The pope on Friday night opened the Holy Door of St. Peter's Basilica to mark the start of the Roman Catholic Church's special Jubilee Year of the Millennium.*

*Pope John Paul II addresses pilgrims and the faithful during his Urbi et Orbi (to the city and the world) message to tens of thousands of people in St. Peter's Square December 25, 1999. The 79-year-old Pontiff issued a clear attack on abortion and called for a ban on the senseless use of weapons. In his message, the Pope said that humanity had much to regret about past centuries and urged the world to look to God's truth to avoid making more mistakes.*

Pope John Paul II appears from his balcony to welcome in the new Millennium January 1, 2000. The 79-year-old Pope, who is fulfilling a personal dream of his papacy by surviving to lead his Church across the threshold of 2000, said he wished that 2000 would be a year of joy and peace.

*Left:* Pope John Paul II is given an assisting hand by President Hosni Mubarak as national anthems finish and the Pope is escorted to greet waiting Egyptian children during his airport welcoming ceremony February 24, 2000. The Pope is on a three day visit to Egypt which will include a mass in Cairo and a visit to St. Catherine's in the Sinai peninsula.

*Pope John Paul II greets Patriarch Astafanous II, head of the Catholic Church in Egypt, on the stage as a mass is held February 25, 2000 in a covered sports stadium. The Pope hammered home an appeal for Christian-Moslem harmony and told worshippers in this predominately Moslem country to build a peaceful society in Egypt and beyond.*

*Pope John Paul II walks under an old olive tree as he waves to the crowd upon entering a garden prayer service at St. Catherine's Greek Orthodox Monastery in the Sinai Desert February 26, 2000. The Pope spoke of the Ten Commandments at the site nearby where Moses received the tablets from God atop Mt. Sinai.*

Pope John Paul II prays close to the cross at the Memorial of Moses Monastery, March 20, 2000. The monastery is built on Mount Nebo and overlooks the Jordan valley and the Jericho oasis. The Pontiff went straight from Amman airport to Mount Nebo where Moses looked across at the land of milk and honey he would never reach. The Pontiff was starting a week-long journey to the Holy Land that he has dreamed of throughout his papacy. It will also take him to Israel and Palestinian-ruled areas.

*Below:* Pope John Paul II holds hands with Palestinian President Yasser Arafat as the President escorts the Roman Catholic Pontiff to his 'Pope Mobile' after his formal welcoming ceremony in Arafat's headquarters in the town where Jesus was born. The Pope continued to Manger Square to deliver a mass meters from the birthplace of Jesus at the Church of the Nativity.

Pope John Paul II sits between Israel's chief Rabbi Meir Lau (L) and Sheikh Tayseer Al-Tamimi, a Moslem cleric, during an inter-religious gathering March 23, 2000 at Jerusalem's Pontifical Institute Notre Dame. Sheikh Tamimi did not shake Rabbi Lau's hand and left the gathering early and did not take part in a symbolic tree planting ceremony. In the background is an image of Jerusalem and the word 'Peace' spelled in Hebrew, Arab and Latin.

**Below:** Pope John Paul II places a large written prayer into a crevice in the stones of the Western Wall as he visits Judaism's holiest site March 26, 2000. The Pope prayed for about two minutes in front of the Wall on the final day of his spiritual historic visit to the Holy Land.

*Pope John Paul II kneels in prayer March 25, 2000 evening at the large stone inside the Basilica of the Agony where the New testament says Jesus prayed at Gethsemani on the night he was arrested before his crucifixion. The Pope is on the penultimate day of his historic visit to the Holy Land and tomorrow will visit sites holy to Moslems, Jews and Christians.*

*Pope John Paul II meets Sister Lucia dos Santos at the holy shrine of Fatima May 13, 2000. Sor Lucia, a frail, 93-year-old nun, is the lone survivor of the three shepherds believed to have had visions of the Madonna in 1917. Pope John Paul said that modern society had to return to traditional values if it wanted to avoid self-destruction.*

*Left: Russian President Vladimir Putin (L) shakes hands with Pope John Paul II during their meeting at the Vatican June 5, 2000. Putin fresh from a summit with U.S. President Bill Clinton, held over two hours of talks with Italian Premier Giuliano Amato on Monday and proposed Europe and NATO erect joint anti-missile defences.*

*Pope John Paul II blesses people beside smiling nuns at the end of his Sunday Angelus in Les Combes July 16, 2000. The 80-year-old Pope arrived on July 10 to rest in Les Combes, a sleepy mountain hamlet near Italy's border with France in the bilingual Val D'Aosta region. For 12 days the Pontiff, who tires more easily than before, will be billeted in a newly built stone house that is part of a summer camp owned by the Salesian religious order.*

*Left Top:* Britain's Queen Elizabeth (L) smiles as she was welcomed by Pope John Paul II before their private audience in Vatican October 17,2000. The Queen, head of the Church of England, returned to the Vatican after 20 years to meet the Pope. The Queen and Prince Philip are on Italy for a four-day visit.

*Left Bottom:* Spanish King Juan Carlos presents a book of an exposition on 16th century Spanish King Charles V to Pope John Paul II during a visit by the King and Queen of Spain to the Vatican November 28, 2000. The Royal couple were received by the Pope in a private audience and later passed through the Holy Door in St. Peter's Basilica during their one-day official visit.

*Below:* Harlem Globetrotters player-coach Curley 'Boo' Johnson (R) gives Pope John Paul II a Globetrotters basketball as assitant coach and player Lou Dunbar (C) looks on during the Pope's weekly general audience in St. Peter's Square November 29, 2000. The Pope, the most travelled Pontiff in history, was made an honorary Harlem Globetrotter in recognition of extroardinary character and achievement, and was presented a team jersey commemorating the 75-year history of the team.

*Pope John Paul II closes St. Peter's basilica Holy Door ending the Catholic Jubilee year January 6, 2001. The 80-year-old Pope closed the door, which is only opened during Holy Years and during which Catholics make pilgrimages to Rome or to their local cathedrals.*

## POPE JOHN PAUL II'S MESSAGE FOR WORLD DAY OF PEACE

January 1, 2001

## "DIALOGUE BETWEEN CULTURES

## FOR A CIVILIZATION OF LOVE AND PEACE"

1. At the dawn of a new millennium, there is growing hope that relationships between people will be increasingly inspired by the ideal of a truly universal brotherhood. Unless this ideal is shared, there will be no way to ensure a stable peace. There are many signs which suggest that this conviction is becoming more deeply rooted in people's minds. The importance of fraternity is proclaimed in the great "charters" of human rights; it is embodied in great international institutions, particularly the United Nations; and it is called for, as never before, by the process of globalization which is leading to a progressive unification of the economy, culture and society. For their part, the followers of the different religions are ever more conscious of the fact that a relationship with the one God, the common Father of all, cannot fail to bring about a greater sense of human brotherhood and a more fraternal life together. In God's revelation in Christ, this principle finds a radical expression: "He who does not love does not know God; for God is love" (1 Jn 4:8).

2. At the same time, however, it cannot be denied that thick clouds overshadow these bright hopes. Humanity is beginning this new chapter of its history with still open wounds. In many regions it is beset by bitter and bloody conflicts, and is struggling with increasing difficulty to maintain solidarity between people of different cultures and civilizations living together in the same territory. We all know how hard it is to settle differences between parties when ancient hatreds and serious problems which admit of no easy solution create an atmosphere of anger and exasperation. But no less dangerous for the future of peace would be the inability to confront intelligently the problems posed by a new social configuration resulting in many countries from accelerated migration and the unprecedented situation of people of different cultures and civilizations living side by side.

3. I therefore consider it urgent to invite believers in Christ, together with all men and women of good will, to reflect on the theme of dialogue between cultures and traditions. This dialogue is the obligatory path to the building of a reconciled world, a world able to look with serenity to its own future. This is a theme which is crucial to the pursuit of peace. I am pleased that the United Nations Organization has called attention to this urgent need by declaring 2001 the "International Year of Dialogue Among Civilizations". Naturally, I do not believe that there can be easy or readily applicable solutions to a problem like this. It is difficult enough to undertake an analysis of the situation, which is in constant flux and defies all preconceived models. There is also the difficulty of combining principles and values which, however reconcilable in the abstract, can prove on the practical level to be resistant to any easy synthesis. In addition, at a deeper level, there are always the demands which ethical commitment makes upon individuals, who are not free of self-interest and human limitations.
But for this very reason I see the usefulness of a shared reflection on these issues. With this intention I confine myself here to offering some guidelines, listening to what the Spirit of God is saying to the Churches (cf. Rev 2:7) and to all of humanity at this decisive hour of its history.
*Mankind and its different cultures*

4. Reflecting upon the human situation, one is always amazed at the complexity and diversity of human cultures. Each of them is distinct by virtue of its specific historical evolution and the resulting characteristics which make it a structurally unique, original and organic whole. Culture is the form of man's self-expression in his journey through history, on the level of both individuals and social groups. For man is driven incessantly by his intellect and will to "cultivate natural goods and values",(1) to incorporate in an ever higher and more systematic cultural synthesis his basic knowledge of all aspects of life, particularly those involving social and political life, security and economic development, and to foster those existential values and perspectives, especially in the religious sphere, which enable individual and community life to develop in a way that is authentically human.(2)

5. A culture is always marked by stable and enduring elements, as well as by changing and contingent features. At first glance, in examining a culture we are struck above all by those aspects which distinguish it from our own culture; these give each culture a face of its own, as an amalgam of quite distinctive elements. In most cases, a culture develops in a specific place, where geographical, historical and ethnic elements combine in an original and unique way. The "uniqueness" of each culture is reflected more or less clearly in those individuals who are its bearers, in a constant process whereby individuals are influenced

by their culture and then, according to their different abilities and genius, contribute to it something of their own. In any event, a person necessarily lives within a specific culture. People are marked by the culture whose very air they breathe through the family and the social groups around them, through education and the most varied influences of their environment, through the very relationship which they have with the place in which they live. There is no determinism here, but rather a constant dialectic between the strength of the individual's conditioning and the workings of human freedom.
*Human development and being part of a culture*

6. The need to accept one's own culture as a structuring element of one's personality, especially in the initial stages of life, is a fact of universal experience whose importance can hardly be overestimated. Without a firm rooting in a specific "soil", individuals risk being subjected at a still vulnerable age to an excess of conflicting stimuli which could impair their serene and balanced development. It is on the basis of this essential relationship with one's own "origins" -- on the level of the family, but also of territory, society and culture -- that people acquire a sense of their nationality, and culture tends to take on, to a greater or lesser degree in different places, a "national" configuration. The Son of God himself, by becoming man, acquired, along with a human family, a country. He remains for ever Jesus of Nazareth, the Nazarean (cf. Mk 10:47; Lk 18:37; Jn 1:45; 19:19). This is a natural process, in which sociological and psychological forces interact, with results that are normally positive and constructive. Love for one's country is thus a value to be fostered, without narrow-mindedness but with love for the whole human family (3) and with an effort to avoid those pathological manifestations which occur when the sense of belonging turns into selfexaltation, the rejection of diversity, and forms of nationalism, racism and xenophobia.

7. Consequently, while it is certainly important to be able to appreciate the values of one's own culture, there is also a need to recognize that every culture, as a typically human and historically conditioned reality, necessarily has its limitations. In order to prevent the sense of belonging to one particular culture from turning into isolation, an effective antidote is a serene and unprejudiced knowledge of other cultures. Moreover, when cultures are carefully and rigorously studied, they very often reveal beneath their outward variations significant common elements. This can also be seen in the historical sequence of cultures and civilizations. The Church, looking to Christ, who reveals man to himself, (4) and drawing upon her experience of two thousand years of history, is convinced that "beneath all that changes, there is much that is unchanging".(5) This continuity is based upon the essential and universal character of God's plan for humanity. Cultural diversity should therefore be understood within the broader horizon of the unity of the human race. In a real way, this unity constitutes the primordial historical and ontological datum in the light of which the profound meaning of cultural diversity can be grasped. In fact, only an overall vision of both the elements of unity and the elements of diversity makes it possible to understand and interpret the full truth of every human culture.(6)
*Cultural differences and mutual respect*

8. In the past, cultural differences have often been a source of misunderstanding between peoples and the cause of conflicts and wars. Even now, sad to say, in different parts of the world we are witnessing with growing alarm the aggressive claims of some cultures against others. In the long run, this situation can end in disastrous tensions and conflicts. At the very least it can make more difficult the situation of those ethnic and cultural minorities living in a majority cultural context which is different from their own and prone to hostile and racist ways of thinking and acting.
In light of this, people of good will need to examine the basic ethical orientations which mark a particular community's cultural experience. Cultures, like the people who give rise to them, are marked by the "mystery of evil" at work in human history (cf. 1 Th 2:7), and they too are in need of purification and salvation. The authenticity of each human culture, the soundness of its underlying ethos, and hence the validity of its moral bearings, can be measured to an extent by its commitment to the human cause and by its capacity to promote human dignity at every level and in every circumstance.

9. The radicalization of identity which makes cultures resistant to any beneficial influence from outside is worrying enough; but no less perilous is the slavish conformity of cultures, or at least of key aspects of them, to cultural models deriving from the Western world. Detached from their Christians origins, these models are often inspired by an approach to life marked by secularism and practical atheism and by patterns of radical individualism. This is a phenomenon of vast proportions, sustained by powerful media campaigns and designed to propagate lifestyles, social and economic programmes and, in the last analysis, a comprehensive world-view which erodes from within other estimable cultures and civilizations. Western cultural models are enticing and alluring because of their remarkable scientific and technical cast, but regrettably there is growing evidence of their deepening human, spiritual and moral impoverishment. The culture which produces such models is marked by the fatal attempt to secure the good of humanity by eliminating God, the Supreme Good. Yet, as the Second Vatican Council warned, "without the Creator the creature comes to nothing!" (7) A culture which no longer has a point of

reference in God loses its soul and loses its way, becoming a culture of death. This was amply demonstrated by the tragic events of the twentieth century and is now apparent in the nihilism present in some prominent circles in the Western world.

## Dialogue between cultures

10. Individuals come to maturity through receptive openness to others and through generous self-giving to them; so too do cultures. Created by people and at the service of people, they have to be perfected through dialogue and communion, on the basis of the original and fundamental unity of the human family as it came from the hands of God who "made from one stock every nation of mankind" (Acts 17:26).

In this perspective, dialogue between cultures -- the theme of this World Day of Peace Message -- emerges as an intrinsic demand of human nature itself, as well as of culture. It is dialogue which protects the distinctiveness of cultures as historical and creative expressions of the underlying unity of the human family, and which sustains understanding and communion between them. The notion of communion, which has its source in Christian revelation and finds its sublime prototype in the Triune God (cf. Jn 17:11, 21), never implies a dull uniformity or enforced homogenization or assimilation; rather it expresses the convergence of a multiform variety, and is therefore a sign of richness and a promise of growth.

Dialogue leads to a recognition of diversity and opens the mind to the mutual acceptance and genuine collaboration demanded by the human family's basic vocation to unity. As such, dialogue is a privileged means for building the civilization of love and peace that my revered predecessor Pope Paul VI indicated as the ideal to inspire cultural, social, political and economic life in our time. At the beginning of the Third Millennium, it is urgent that the path of dialogue be proposed once again to a world marked by excessive conflict and violence, a world at times discouraged and incapable of seeing signs of hope and peace.

## Possibilities and risks of global communication

11. Dialogue between cultures is especially needed today because of the impact of new communications technology on the lives of individuals and peoples. Ours is an era of global communication, which is shaping society along the lines of new cultural models which more or less break with past models. At least in principle, accurate and up-todate information is available to anyone in any part of the world.

The free flow of images and speech on a global scale is transforming not only political and economic relations between peoples, but even our understanding of the world. It opens up a range of hitherto unthinkable possibilities, but it also has certain negative and dangerous aspects. The fact that a few countries have a monopoly on these cultural "industries" and distribute their products to an ever growing public in every corner of the earth can be a powerful factor in undermining cultural distinctness. These products include and transmit implicit value-systems and can therefore lead to a kind of dispossession and loss of cultural identity in those who receive them.

## The challenge of migration

12. A style and culture of dialogue are especially important when it comes to the complex question of migration, which is an important social phenomenon of our time. The movement of large numbers of people from one part of the planet to another is often a terrible odyssey for those involved, and it brings with it the intermingling of traditions and customs, with notable repercussions both on the countries from which people come and on those in which they settle. How migrants are welcomed by receiving countries and how well they become integrated in their new environment are also an indication of how much effective dialogue there is between the various cultures.

The question of cultural integration is much debated these days, and it is not easy to specify in detail how best to guarantee, in a balanced and equitable way, the rights and duties of those who welcome and those who are welcomed. Historically, migrations have occurred in all sorts of ways and with very different results. In the case of many civilizations, immigration has brought new growth and enrichment. In other cases, the local people and immigrants have remained culturally separate but have shown that they are able to live together, respecting each other and accepting or tolerating the diversity of customs. Regrettably, situations still exist in which the difficulties involved in the encounter of different cultures have never been resolved, and the consequent tensions have become the cause of periodic outbreaks of conflict.

13. In such a complex issue there are no "magic" formulas; but still we must identify some basic ethical principles to serve as points of reference. First of all, it is important to remember the principle that immigrants must always be treated with the respect due to the dignity of every human person. In the matter of controlling the influx of immigrants, the consideration which should rightly be given to the common good should not ignore this principle. The challenge is to combine the welcome due to every human being, especially

when in need, with a reckoning of what is necessary for both the local inhabitants and the new arrivals to live a dignified and peaceful life. The cultural practices which immigrants bring with them should be respected and accepted, as long as they do not contravene either the universal ethical values inherent in the natural law or fundamental human rights.

## Respect for cultures and the "cultural profile" of different regions

14. It is a much more difficult thing to determine the extent to which immigrants are entitled to public legal recognition of the particular customs of their culture, which may not be readily compatible with the customs of the majority of citizens. The solution to this question, within a climate of genuine openness, calls for a realistic evaluation of the common good at any given time in history and in any given place and social context. Much depends upon whether people embrace a spirit of openness that, without yielding to indifferentism about values, can combine the concern for identity with the willingness to engage in dialogue.

On the other hand, as I noted above, one cannot underestimate the capacity of the characteristic culture of a region to produce a balanced growth, especially in the delicate early stages of life, in those who belong to that culture from birth. From this point of view, a reasonable way forward would be to ensure a certain "cultural equilibrium" in each region, by reference to the culture which has prevalently marked its development. This equilibrium, even while welcoming minorities and respecting their basic rights, would allow the continued existence and development of a particular "cultural profile", by which I mean that basic heritage of language, traditions and values which are inextricably part of a nation's history and its national identity.

15. Clearly, though, the need to ensure an equilibrium in a region's cultural profile cannot be met by legislative measures alone, since these would prove ineffectual unless they were grounded in the ethos of the population. They would also be inevitably destined to change should a culture lose its ability to inspire a people and a region, becoming no more than a legacy preserved in museums or in artistic and literary monuments. In effect, as long as a culture is truly alive, it need have no fear of being displaced. And no law could keep it alive if it were already dead in people's hearts. In the dialogue between cultures, no side can be prevented from proposing to the other the values in which it believes, as long as this is done in way that is respectful of people's freedom and conscience. "Truth can be imposed only with the force of truth itself, which penetrates the mind both gently and powerfully". (8)

## The recognition of shared values

16. Dialogue between cultures, a privileged means for building the civilization of love, is based upon the recognition that there are values which are common to all cultures because they are rooted in the nature of the person. These values express humanity's most authentic and distinctive features. Leaving aside ideological prejudices and selfish interests, it is necessary to foster people's awareness of these shared values, in order to nurture that intrinsically universal cultural "soil" which makes for fruitful and constructive dialogue. The different religions too can and ought to contribute decisively to this process. My many encounters with representatives of other religions -- I recall especially the meeting in Assisi in 1986 and in Saint Peter's Square in 1999 -- have made me more confident that mutual openness between the followers of the various religions can greatly serve the cause of peace and the common good of the human family.

## The value of solidarity

17. Faced with growing inequalities in the world, the prime value which must be ever more widely inculcated is certainly that of solidarity. A society depends on the basic relations that people cultivate with one another in ever widening circles -- from the family to other intermediary social groups, to civil society as a whole and to the national community. States in turn have no choice but to enter into relations with one another. The present reality of global interdependence makes it easier to appreciate the common destiny of the entire human family, and makes all thoughtful people increasingly appreciate the virtue of solidarity.

At the same time it is necessary to point out that this growing interdependence has brought to light many inequalities, such as the gap between rich and poor nations; the social imbalance within each nation between those living in opulence and those offended in their dignity since they lack even the necessities of life; the human and environmental degradation provoked and accelerated by the irresponsible use of natural resources. These social inequalities and imbalances have grown worse in certain places, and some of the poorest nations have reached a point of irreversible decline.

Consequently, the promotion of justice is at the heart of a true culture of solidarity. It is not just a question of giving one's surplus to those in need, but of "helping entire peoples presently excluded or marginalized to enter into the sphere of economic and human development. For this to happen, it is not enough to draw on the surplus goods which in fact our world abundantly produces; it requires above all a change of lifestyles, of models of production and consumption, and of the established structures of power which today govern societies". (9)

## The value of peace

18. The culture of solidarity is closely connected with the value of peace, the primary objective of every society and of national and international life. However, on the path to better understanding among peoples there remain many challenges which the world must face: these set before everyone choices which cannot be postponed. The alarming increase of arms, together with the halting progress of commitment to nuclear non-proliferation, runs the risk of feeding and expanding a culture of competition and conflict, a culture involving not only States but also non-institutional entities, such as paramilitary groups and terrorist organizations.

Even today the world is dealing with the consequences of wars past and present, as well as the tragic effects of anti-personnel mines and the use of frightful chemical and biological weapons. And what can be said about the permanent risk of conflicts between nations, of civil wars within some States and of widespread violence, before which international organizations and national governments appear almost impotent? Faced with such threats, everyone must feel the moral duty to take concrete and timely steps to promote the cause of peace and understanding among peoples.

## The value of life

19. An authentic dialogue between cultures cannot fail to nourish, in addition to sentiments of mutual respect, a lively sense of the value of life itself. Human life cannot be seen as an object to do with as we please, but as the most sacred and inviolable earthly reality. There can be no peace when this most basic good is not protected. It is not possible to invoke peace and despise life. Our own times have seen shining examples of generosity and dedication in the service of life, but also the sad sight of hundreds of millions of men and women whom cruelty and indifference have consigned to a painful and harsh destiny. I am speaking of a tragic spiral of death which includes murder, suicide, abortion, euthanasia, as well as practices of mutilation, physical and psychological torture, forms of unjust coercion, arbitrary imprisonment, unnecessary recourse to the death penalty, deportations, slavery, prostitution, trafficking in women and children. To this list we must add irresponsible practices of genetic engineering, such as the cloning and use of human embryos for research, which are justified by an illegitimate appeal to freedom, to cultural progress, to the advancement of mankind. When the weakest and most vulnerable members of society are subjected to such atrocities, the very idea of the human family, built on the value of the person, on trust, respect and mutual support, is dangerously eroded. A civilization based on love and peace must oppose these experiments, which are unworthy of man.

## The value of education

20. In order to build the civilization of love, dialogue between cultures must work to overcome all ethnocentric selfishness and make it possible to combine regard for one's own identity with understanding of others and respect for diversity. Fundamental in this respect is the responsibility of education. Education must make students aware of their own roots and provide points of reference which allow them to define their own personal place in the world. At the same time, it must be committed to teaching respect for other cultures. There is a need to look beyond one's immediate personal experience and accept differences, discovering the richness to be found in other people's history and in their values. Knowledge of other cultures, acquired with an appropriate critical sense and within a solid ethical framework, leads to a deeper awareness of the values and limitations within one's own culture, and at the same time it reveals the existence of a patrimony that is common to the whole of humanity. Thanks precisely to this broadening of horizons, education has a particular role to play in building a more united and peaceful world. It can help to affirm that integral humanism, open to life's ethical and religious dimension, which appreciates the importance of understanding and showing esteem for other cultures and the spiritual values present in them.

## Forgiveness and reconciliation

21. During the Great Jubilee, two thousand years after the birth of Jesus, the Church has had a powerful experience of the challenging call to reconciliation. This call is significant also in the context of the complex issue of dialogue between cultures. Dialogue in fact is often difficult because it is weighed down by the tragic heritage of war, conflict, violence and hatred, which lives on in people's memory. For the barriers caused by noncommunication to be bridged, the path to take is the path of forgiveness and reconciliation. Many people, in the name of a disillusioned realism, maintain that this

is a utopian and naive path. From the Christian point of view it is the only path which leads to the goal of peace.

The eyes of believers contemplate the image of the Crucified One. Shortly before dying, Jesus exclaims: "Father, forgive them, for they know not what they do" (Lk 23:34). The evil-doer crucified on his right, hearing these last words of the dying Redeemer, opens his heart to the grace of conversion, welcomes the Gospel of forgiveness and receives the promise of eternal happiness. The example of Christ makes us certain that the many impediments to communication and dialogue between people can indeed be torn down. Gazing upon the Crucified One we are filled with confidence that forgiveness and reconciliation can become the normal practice of everyday life and of every culture, and thus a real opportunity for building humanity's peace and future. Mindful of the significant Jubilee experience of the purification of memory, I wish to make a specific appeal to Christians to become witnesses to and missionaries of forgiveness and reconciliation. In this way, through their active invocation of the God of peace, they will hasten the fulfilment of Isaiah's splendid prophecy, which can be applied to all the peoples of the earth: "In that day there will be a highway from Egypt to Assyria, and the Assyrian will come into Egypt, and the Egyptian into Assyria, and the Egyptians will worship with the Assyrians. In that day Israel will be the third with Egypt and Assyria, a blessing in the midst of the earth, whom the Lord of hosts has blessed, saying, 'Blessed be Egypt my people, and Assyria the work of my hands, and Israel my heritage'" (Is 19:23-25).

## An appeal to young people

22. I wish to conclude this Message of peace with a special appeal to you, young people of the whole world, who are humanity's future and living stones in the building of the civilization of love. I treasure in my heart the memory of the emotional and hope-filled meetings which we had during the recent World Youth Day in Rome. Your participation was joyous, sincere and reassuring. In your energy and vitality, and in your love of Christ, I was able to glimpse a more peaceful and human future for the world.

Feeling your closeness to me, I sensed a profound gratitude to the Lord who gave me the grace of contemplating - through the multicoloured mosaic of your different languages, cultures, customs and ways of thinking - the miracle of the universality of the Church, of her catholicity, of her unity. Through you I was able to admire the marvellous coming together of diversity in the unity of the same faith, the same hope, the same love. Here was an eloquent expression of the wondrous reality of the Church, sign and instrument of Christ for the salvation of the world and for the unity of mankind. (10) The Gospel calls you to rebuild the original unity of the human family, which has its source in God the Father, Son and Holy Spirit. Dear young people of every language and culture, a high and exhilarating task awaits you: that of becoming men and women capable of solidarity, peace and love of life, with respect for everyone. Become craftsmen of a new humanity, where brothers and sisters - members all of the same family - are able at last to live in peace.

## "The Word 'Peace' Echoes in Our Hearts"
## Papal Address at Airport in Damascus

MAY 6, 2001

*Mr President, Members of the Government, Brother Patriarchs and Bishops, Distinguished Ladies and Gentlemen,*

*1. As I arrive in Damascus, this "pearl of the East", I am deeply aware that I am visiting a very ancient land, which has played a vital role in the history of this part of the world. Syria's literary, artistic and social contribution to the flourishing of culture and civilization is renowned. I am most grateful to you, Mr President, and to the Members of the Government, for making my visit to Syria possible, and I thank you for your kind words of welcome. I greet the civil, political and military Authorities graciously present, as well as the distinguished members of the Diplomatic Corps.*
*I come as a pilgrim of faith, continuing my Jubilee Pilgrimage to some of the places especially connected with God's self-revelation and his saving actions (cf. Letter Concerning Pilgrimage to the Places Linked to the History of Salvation,*

*1). Today he allows me to continue this pilgrimage here, in Syria, in Damascus, and to greet all of you in friendship and brotherhood. I greet the Patriarchs and Bishops who are here, representing the Syrian Christian community. My heartfelt greeting goes to all the followers of Islam who live in this noble land. Peace be with you all! As-salāmu 'alāikum!*

*2. My Jubilee Pilgrimage marking the two thousandth anniversary of the birth of Jesus Christ actually began last year, with the commemoration of Abraham, to whom God's call came not far from here in the region of Haran. Later, I was able to travel to Mount Sinai, where the Ten Commandments were given to Moses. And then there was my unforgettable visit to the Holy Land, where Jesus fulfilled his saving mission and founded his Church. Now my mind and heart turn to the figure of Saul of Tarsus, the great Apostle Paul, whose life was changed for ever on the road to Damascus. My ministry as Bishop of Rome is linked in a special way to the witness of Saint Paul, a witness crowned by his martyrdom in Rome.*

*3. How can I forget the magnificent contribution of Syria and the surrounding region to the history of Christianity? From the very beginning of Christianity, flourishing communities were to be found here. In the Syrian desert Christian monasticism flourished; and the names of Syrians such as Saint Ephraem and Saint John Damascene are etched for ever in Christian memory. Some of my predecessors were born in this area.*
*I am thinking too of the great cultural influence of Syrian Islam, which under the Umayyad Caliphs reached the farthest shores of the Mediterranean. Today, in a world that is increasingly complex and interdependent, there is a need for a new spirit of dialogue and cooperation between Christians and Muslims. Together we acknowledge the one indivisible God, the Creator of all that exists. Together we must proclaim to the world that the name of the one God is "a name of peace and a summons to peace" (Novo millennio ineunte, 55)!*

*4. As the word "peace" echoes in our hearts, how can we not think of the tensions and conflicts which have long troubled the region of the Middle East? So often hopes for peace have been raised, only to be dashed by new waves of violence. You, Mr President, have wisely confirmed that a just and global peace is in the best interests of Syria. I am confident that under your guidance Syria will spare no effort to work for greater harmony and cooperation among the peoples of the region, in order to bring lasting benefits not only to your own land, but also to other Arab countries and the whole international community. As I have publicly stated on other occasions, it is time to "return to the principles of international legality: the banning of the acquisition of territory by force, the right of peoples to self-determination, respect for the resolutions of the United Nations Organization and the Geneva conventions, to quote only the most important" (Speech to the Diplomatic Corps accredited to the Holy See, 13 January 2001, No. 3).*
*We all know that real peace can only be achieved if there is a new attitude of understanding and respect between the peoples of the region, between the followers of the*

*three Abrahamic religions. Step by step, with vision and courage, the political and religious leaders of the region must create the conditions for the development that their peoples have a right to, after so much conflict and suffering. Among these conditions, it is important that there be an evolution in the way the peoples of the region see one another, and that at every level of society the principles of peaceful coexistence be taught and promoted. In this sense, my pilgrimage is also an ardent prayer of hope: hope that among the peoples of the region fear will turn to trust; and contempt to mutual esteem; that force will give way to dialogue; and that a genuine desire to serve the common good will prevail.*

*5. Mr President, the gracious invitation which you and the Government and people of Syria have extended to me, and the warmth of your welcome here today, are signs of our shared belief that peace and cooperation are indeed our common aspiration. I deeply appreciate your hospitality, so characteristic of this ancient and blessed land. May Almighty God grant you happiness and long life! May he bless Syria with prosperity and peace! As-salāmu 'alāikum!*

*Left: Syrian President Bashar al-Assad reaches for Pope John Paul II before they start reviewing troops at Damascus airport May 5, 2001. Pope John Paul began a pilgrimage to Syria today with a call to feuding parties in the Arab-Israeli conflict to seek a lasting peace in the troubled Middle East. Syria is the second leg of a six-day tour to retrace the steps of St Paul in Greece, Syria and Malta.*

*Pope John Paul II watches a child during a closing mass of a four-day special consistory in St. Peter's Basilica May 24, 2001. More than 150 of the globes 183 cardinals convereged in the Vatican for the consistory meeting, with the theme Pastoral Perspectives of the Church in the Third Millennium.*

*Pope John Paul II sits and rests during his holidays in the mountain resort of Les Combes, northern Italy in this July 19, 2001 file picture. Pope John Paul II urged the leaders of the Group of Eight industrialised nations to make their meeting a sign of solidarity for the world, particularly the poor.*

*U.S. President George W. Bush reads a statement as Pope John Paul II listens at the Pope's country retreat, Castelgandolfo, July 23, 2001. During the statements, the Pope commented on the growing debate over stem cell research in the medical profession.*

## John Paul II's Address to Bush at Castel Gandolfo
## "America ... Has a Special Responsibility"

JULY 23, 2001

It gives me great pleasure to welcome you on your first visit since you assumed the office of President of the United States.

I warmly greet the distinguished first lady and the members of your entourage.

I express heartfelt good wishes that your presidency will strengthen your country in its commitment to the principles which inspired American democracy from the beginning, and sustained the nation in its remarkable growth.

These principles remain as valid as ever, as you face the challenges of the new century opening up before us.

Your nation's founders, conscious of the immense natural and human resources with which your land had been blessed by the Creator, were guided by a profound sense of responsibility towards the common good, to be pursued in respect for the God-given dignity and inalienable rights of all.

America continues to measure herself by the nobility of her founding vision in building a society of liberty, equality and justice under the law.

In the century which has just ended, these same ideals inspired the American people to resist two totalitarian systems based on an atheistic vision of man and society.

At the beginning of this new century, which also marks the beginning of the third millennium of Christianity, the world continues to look to America with hope.

Yet it does so with an acute awareness of the crisis of values being experienced in Western society, ever more insecure in the face of the ethical decisions indispensable for humanity's future course.

In recent days, the world's attention has been focused on the process of globalisation which has so greatly accelerated in the past decade, and which you and other leaders of the industrialised nations have discussed in Genoa.

While appreciating the opportunities for economic growth and material prosperity which this process offers, the Church cannot but express profound concern that our world continues to be divided, no longer by the former political and military blocs, but by a tragic fault line between those who can benefit from these opportunities and those who seem cut off from them.

The revolution of freedom of which I spoke at the United Nations in 1995 must now be completed by a revolution of opportunity, in which all the world's peoples actively contribute to economic prosperity and share in its fruits.

This requires leadership by those nations whose religious and cultural traditions should make them most attentive to the moral dimension of the issues involved.

Respect for human dignity and belief in the equal dignity of all the members of the human family demand policies aimed at enabling all peoples to have access to the means required to improve their lives, including the technological means and skills needed for development.

Respect for nature by everyone, a policy of openness to immigrants, the cancellation or significant reduction of the debt of poorer nations, the promotion of peace through dialogue and negotiation, the primacy of the rule of law: these are the priorities which the leaders of the developed nations cannot disregard.

A global world is essentially a world of solidarity! From this point of view, America, because of her many resources, cultural traditions and religious values, has a special responsibility.

Respect for human dignity finds one of its highest expressions in religious freedom. This right is the first listed in your nation's Bill of Rights, and it is significant that the promotion of religious freedom continues to be an important goal of American policy in the international community.

I gladly express the appreciation of the whole Catholic Church for America's commitment in this regard.

Another area in which political and moral choices have the gravest consequences for the future of civilisation concerns the most fundamental of human rights, the right to life itself.

Experience is already showing how a tragic coarsening of consciences accompanies the assault on innocent human life in the womb, leading to accommodation and acquiescence in the face of other related evils such as euthanasia, infanticide and, most recently, proposals for the creation for research purposes of human embryos, destined to destruction in the process. A free and virtuous society, which America aspires to be, must reject practices that devalue and violate human life at any stage from conception until natural death.

In defending the right to life, in law and through a vibrant culture of life, America can show the world the path to a truly humane future, in which man remains the master, not the product, of his technology. Mr. President, as you carry out the tasks of the high office which the American people have entrusted to you, I assure you of a remembrance in my prayers.

I am confident that under your leadership your nation will continue to draw on its heritage and resources to help build a world in which each member of the human family can flourish and live in a manner worthy of his or her innate dignity.

With these sentiments I cordially invoke upon you and the beloved American people Gods blessings of wisdom, strength and peace.

Kyazim Azizov, who calls himself 'The Prince of the World' (R) stands on crutches as he receives the blessing of Pope John Paul II (L) at the end of a mass in Baku May 23, 2002. Earlier Azizov, 40, had clambered on to the stage and got within 10 feet (three metres) of the Pontiff but was quickly led away. After a few minutes of confusion and questioning by Azeri and Vatican officials, Aziziv - who claimed to be a visionary - was deemed harmless and was released. At the end of the mass he was allowed to approach the Pope and kiss his hand.

**Right:** Pope John Paul II is helped by a bishop to board a helicopter on his return to Ciampino airport from Bulgaria May 26, 2002. Pope John Paul returned from the 96th foreign tour of his pontificate on Sunday, after a five-day trip to Azerbaijan and Bulgaria.

*Georgia Giddings from Baysville, Ontario, cries after meeting Pope John Paul II (L) following his arrival in Toronto, July 23, 2002.*

## John Paul II's Address Upon Arrival in Toronto "Values that Are Essential to Good Living and Human Happiness"

JULY 23, 2002

*Dear Prime Minister Chrétien,*
*Dear Canadian Friends,*

1. I am deeply grateful for your words of welcome, Mr. Prime Minister, and feel greatly honored by the presence here of the Premier of Ontario, the Mayor of the great city of Toronto, and other distinguished representatives of government and civil society. To all I say a resounding "thank you" for welcoming the idea of holding the World Youth Day in Canada and for all that has been done to make it a reality.
Dear People of Canada, I have vivid memories of my first apostolic visit in 1984, and of my brief visit in 1987 to the First Nations in the land of Denendeh. This time I must be content to stay only in Toronto. From here I greet all Canadians. You are in my thankful prayers to God, who has so abundantly blessed your vast and beautiful country.

2. Young people from all parts of the world are gathering for the World Youth Day. With their gifts of intelligence and heart they represent the future of the world. But they also bear the marks of a humanity that too often does not know peace, or justice. Too many lives begin and end without joy, without hope. That is one of the principal reasons for the World Youth Day. Young people are coming together to commit themselves, in the strength of their faith in Jesus Christ, to the great cause of peace and human solidarity.
Thank you, Toronto; thank you, Canada, for welcoming them with open arms!

3. In the French version of your national anthem, "O Canada", you sing: "Car ton bras sait porter l'épée, il sait porter la croix ..." Canadians are heirs to an extraordinarily rich humanism, enriched even more by the blend of many different cultural elements. But the core of your heritage is the spiritual and transcendent vision of life based on Christian revelation which gave vital impetus to your development as a free, democratic and caring society, recognized throughout the world as a champion of human rights and human dignity.

4. In a world of great social and ethical strains, and confusion about the very purpose of life, Canadians have an incomparable treasure to contribute -- on condition that they preserve what is deep, and good and valid in their own heritage. I pray that the World Youth Day will offer all Canadians an opportunity to remember the values that are essential to good living and to human happiness.

Mr. Prime Minister, dear Friends: may the motto of the World Youth Day echo throughout the land, reminding all Christians to be "salt of the earth and light of the world".

God bless you all. God bless Canada.

*Canadian Prime Minister Jean Chretien kisses the hand of Pope John Paul II following the Pontiff's arrival in Toronto, July 23, 2002. The Pope is in Canada to participate in World Youth Day.*

*Mexican President Vicente Fox talks with Pope John Paul II during the Pope's arrival ceremony in Mexico City July 30, 2002. A tired Pope John Paul II arrived in Mexico on Tuesday, where he will make a 16th Century peasant Latin America's first Indian saint on the last leg of an 11-day tour in which he has reached out to indigenous people.*

### John Paul II's Address on Arrival in Mexico

### "May God Make You Like Juan Diego!"

JULY 31, 2002

*Mr. President of the United Mexican States, Your Eminence, the Cardinal Archbishop of Mexico City, Dear Brothers in the Episcopate, Distinguished Authorities and Members of the Diplomatic Corps,*

*Dear Mexican People,*

*1. I am filled with great joy at being able to come to this hospitable land for the fifth time. It was here that I began my Apostolic travels which have taken me as the Successor of the Apostle Peter to so many parts of the world, bringing me close to many men and women to strengthen them in their faith in our Savior, Jesus Christ.*
*After celebrating the 17th World Youth Day in Toronto, today I have had the good fortune to add to the list of saints a wonderful evangelizer from this continent: Brother Pedro de San José de Betancur. Tomorrow, with deep joy I shall canonize Juan Diego, and on the following day I shall beatify two other compatriots of yours: Juan Bautista and Jacinto de los Angeles, who will thus join these beautiful examples of holiness in these beloved American countries, where the Christian message has been welcomed with open hearts, permeating their cultures and bringing forth abundant fruit.*

*2. I am grateful for the friendly words of welcome which the President has addressed to me on behalf of all Mexicans. I would like to reciprocate by renewing once more my sentiments of affection and esteem for this people with their wealth of history and ancestral cultures. I encourage everybody to work for the building up of an ever renewed homeland and for the country's continual progress. I greet with affection the Cardinals and Bishops, the dear priests, men and women religious, all the faithful who day by day endeavor to practice the Christian faith and make the words that are the hope and program of the future come true: "Mexico ever faithful!". From here I also send an affectionate greeting to the young people gathered at a prayer vigil in Plaza del Zócalo in front of the Primatial Cathedral, and I tell them that the Pope is counting on them and asking them to be true friends of Jesus and witnesses to his Gospel.*

*3. Dear Mexicans: thank you for your hospitality, for your constant affection, for your fidelity to the Church. Continue to be faithful on this journey, encouraged by the marvelous examples of holiness born in this noble nation. Be holy! Repeating what I said to you in the Basilica of Guadalupe in 1990, serve God, the Church and the nation, each one assuming personal responsibility for passing on the Gospel message and witnessing to a faith that is alive and active in society.*
*I cordially bless each one of you, with the words which your ancestors addressed to their loved ones: "May God make you like Juan Diego!"*

Pope John Paul II blesses the bones of one of two Mexican indigenous martyrs he beatified during mass in the Basilica of the Virgin of Guadalupe in Mexico City August 1, 2002. The Pope celebrated mass to beatify Juan Batista and Jacinto de los Angeles, two indigenous Mexican martyrs from the southern Mexican state of Oaxaca.

**Right:** A Mexican indian woman waves an orange branch over Pope John Paul II as she performs a traditional spirtual cleansing ceremony on him, during mass in the Basilica of the Virgin of Guadalupe in Mexico City, August 1, 2002. A weaker and fatigued Pope on Thursday concludes one of the longest trips of his pontificate, returning to Rome from the country where he began his foreign travels more than two decades ago. The 82-year-old pontiff is scheduled to leave Mexico after beatifying two Indians who were lynched in 1700 after denouncing their Indian community to Catholic authorities for worshiping pagan idols.

*Pope John Paul II waves to well wishers with unidentified priests behind him upon his arrival at Balice airport in Krakow, southern Poland August 16, 2002. The 82 year-old Pontiff arived in Poland for his ninth pilgrimage to his homeland on a four-day visit.*

*A pilgrim waves to Pope John Paul II as he arrives in St Peter's square for the canonisation ceremony of Spanish priest Josemaria Escrivan de Balaguer October 6, 2002. Escriva, founder of the conservative Catholic group Opus Dei, is the 468th saint proclaimed by the Pope, who has made more saints than all of his predecessors in the last four centuries combined.*

*Pope John Paul II waves in St. Peters's Square after he delivered his Urbi et Orbi (to the city and the world) message December 25, 2002. A frail Pope appealed in his Christmas message to the world to avoid a conflict in Iraq. Speaking in a trembling and hoarse voice on a cold day, the 82-year-old Pontiff made his appeal for peace in the Middle East.*

**Below:** *Pope John Paul II gestures as he chats with United Nations Secretary General Kofi Annan during a private meeting at the Pope's library in the Vatican February 18, 2003. Both the Pope and Anan agreed that the U.N. was essential to solving the Iraqi crisis.*

*Pope John Paul II has an audience with Prime Minister Tony Blair during his first visit to the Pope in the library at the Vatican February 22, 2003. Faced with fervent opposition in Britain to U.S.-led military action on Iraq, Blair became the latest world leader to visit the pontiff to discuss the crisis over Iraq. The Vatican has refused to bless a possible U.S.-led attack on Iraq as a just war.*

## Vatican Statement on Pope's Meeting with Tony Blair Solution to Iraqi Crisis Must "Spare the World New Divisions"

FEB. 23, 2003

This morning, Saturday, Feb. 22, 2003, the Holy Father received in private audience H.E. Mr. Tony Blair, Prime Minister of Great Britain. In the course of the cordial conversation, which lasted a half hour, there was talk of the complex international juncture, with particular reference to the Middle East. The Holy Father hoped that, in the solution of the grave situation in Iraq, every effort will be made to spare the world new divisions.

Subsequently, the Holy Father received Mr. Blair's family.

The Prime Minister of Great Britain also met with Cardinal Angelo Sodano, secretary of state, who received him together with H.E. Archbishop Jean-Louis Tauran, secretary for relations with states.

In this morning's talks in the Vatican the need was emphasized that all interested parties in the noted Iraqi crisis might collaborate with the United Nations and know how to make use of the resources offered by international law, to avert the tragedy of a war that from different sides is still believed to be avoidable. Special consideration was given to the humanitarian situation of the Iraqi people, already harshly tried by long years of embargo.

In the course of the meetings, there was also an exchange of opinions on the future Constitutional Treaty of Europe. On the part of the Holy See, the hope was expressed for explicit recognition of the Churches and communities of believers as well as for a commitment of the European Union to maintain a structured dialogue with them.

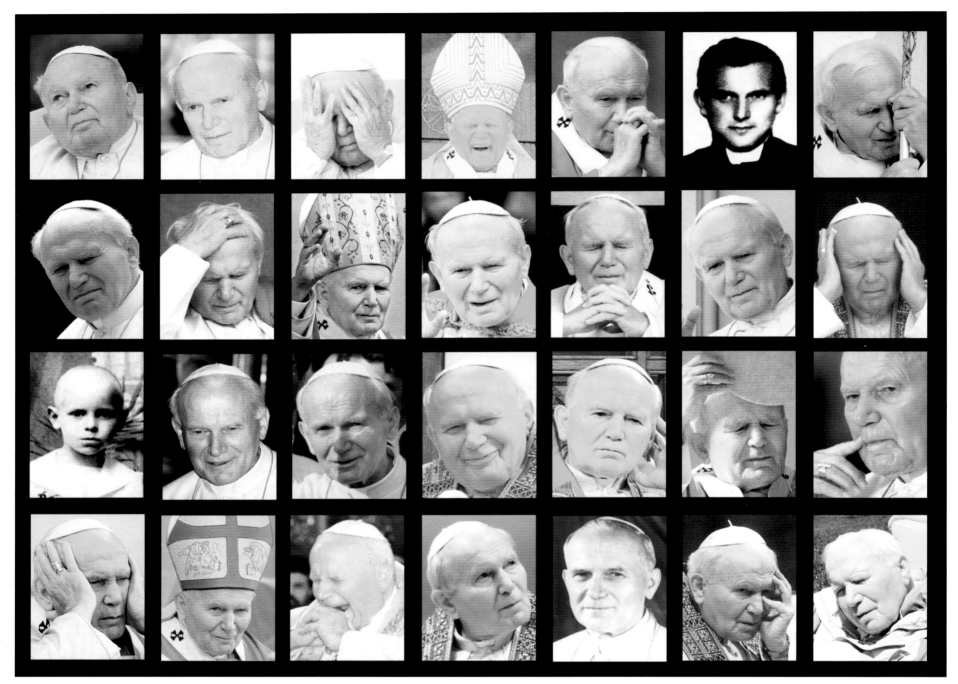

*A combination photo shows file pictures of Pope John Paul II throughout his life. The Pontiff celebrated his 84th birthday on May 18, 2004 with the publication of his new book, 'Get up. Let us go!', recalling his life from youth to old age.*

## John Paul II's Address to President of U.N. General Assembly

FEB. 8, 2004

Mr. President,

I am pleased to welcome you to the Vatican in your capacity as the President of the 58th General Assembly of the United Nations.

As you know, the Holy See considers the United Nations Organization a significant means for promoting the universal common good. You have undertaken a restructuring aimed at making the Organization function more efficiently. This will not only ensure an effective superior instance for the just resolution of international problems, but also enable the United Nations to become an ever more highly respected moral authority for the international community.

It is my hope that the Member States will consider such a reform "a clear moral and political obligation which calls for prudence and determination" (Message for the 2004 World Day of Peace, 7), and a necessary prerequisite for the growth of an international order at the service of the whole human family.

I offer prayerful good wishes for your own efforts on behalf of this goal and I willingly invoke upon you and your associates the divine blessings of wisdom, strength and peace.

## John Paul II's Easter Message

## "The Strength to Face the Phenomenon of Terrorism"

APRIL 11, 2004

1. "'Resurrexit,' alleluia -- He is risen, alleluia!" This year too the joyous proclamation of Easter, which echoed powerfully at last night's vigil, strengthens our hope. "Why do you seek the living among the dead? He is not here, but has risen" (Luke 24:5-6). Thus the angel encourages the women who have hastened to the tomb. Thus the Easter liturgy repeats to us, the men and women of the third millennium: Christ is risen, Christ is alive among us! His name now is "the Living One," death has no more power over him (cf. Romans 6:9).

2. "Resurrexit!" Today you, O Redeemer of mankind, rise victoriously from the tomb to offer to us, troubled by many threatening shadows, your wish for joy and peace. Those who are tempted by anxiety and desperation turn to you, O Christ, our life and our guide, to hear the proclamation of the hope that does not disappoint. On this day of your victory over death, may humanity find in you, O Lord, the courage to oppose in solidarity the many evils that afflict it. In particular, may it find the strength to face the inhuman, and unfortunately growing, phenomenon of terrorism, which rejects life and brings anguish and uncertainty to the daily lives of so many hardworking and peaceful people. May your wisdom enlighten men and women of good will in the required commitment against this scourge.

3. May the work of national and international institutions hasten the overcoming of the present difficulties and favor progress toward a more effective and peaceful world order. May world leaders be confirmed and sustained in their efforts to resolve satisfactorily the continuing conflicts that cause bloodshed in certain regions of Africa, Iraq and the Holy

Land. You, firstborn of many brothers, grant that all who consider themselves children of Abraham may rediscover the brotherhood that they share and that prompts in them designs of cooperation and peace.

4. Take heed all of you who have at heart mankind's future! Take heed men and women of good will! May the temptation to seek revenge give way to the courage to forgive; may the culture of life and love render vain the logic of death; may trust once more give breath to the lives of peoples. If our future is one, it is the task and duty of all to build it with patient and painstaking farsightedness.

5. "Lord, to whom shall we go?" You who have conquered death, you alone "have the words of eternal life" (John 6:68). To you we raise with confidence our prayer which becomes an invocation of comfort for the families of the many victims of violence. Help us to work ceaselessly for the coming of that more just and united world that you have inaugurated with your resurrection. Accompanying us in this task is "she who believed that there would be a fulfillment of what was spoken to her from the Lord" (Luke 1:45). Blessed are you, O Mary, silent witness of Easter! You, O Mother of the Crucified One now risen, who at the hour of pain and death kept the flame of hope burning, teach us also to be, among the incongruities of passing time, convinced and joyful witnesses of the eternal message of life and love brought to the world by the Risen Redeemer.

## George Bush's Address to John Paul II

## "We Will Work for Human Liberty and Human Dignity"

### JUNE 4, 2004

Your Holiness,
Thank you very much for receiving Laura and me and our delegation.
I bring greetings from our country, where you are respected, admired and greatly loved. I also bring a message from my government that says to you, Sir, that we will work for human liberty and human dignity in order to spread peace and compassion; that we appreciate the strong symbol of freedom that you have stood for, and we recognize the power of freedom to change societies and to change the world.
And so, Sir, we are honored to be here; perhaps the best way I can express my country's gratitude to you and our respect to you is to present to you the Medal of Freedom from America and, if you might, allow, I'd like to read the citation attached to that honor.
"A devoted servant of God, His Holiness Pope John Paul II has championed the cause of the poor, the weak, the hungry, and the outcast.
"He has defended the unique dignity of every life, and the goodness of all life.
"Through his faith and moral conviction, he has given courage to others to 'be not afraid' in overcoming injustice and oppression.
"His principled stand for peace and freedom has inspired millions and helped to topple Communism and tyranny.
"The United States honors this son of Poland who became the Bishop of Rome, and a hero of our time."

## Papal Telegram to Nancy Reagan

### JUNE 8, 2004

To Mrs. Nancy Reagan
Having learned with sadness of the death of President Reagan I offer to you and your family my heartfelt condolences and the assurance of my prayers for his eternal rest. I recall with deep gratitude the late president's unwavering commitment to the service of the nation and to the cause of freedom as well as his abiding faith in the human and spiritual values which ensure a future of solidarity, justice and peace in our world. Together with your family and the American people I commend his noble soul to the merciful love of God our heavenly Father and cordially invoke upon all who mourn his passing the divine blessings of consolation, strength and peace.

Ioannes Paulus PP. II

*President George W. Bush (L) and his wife Laura (R) greets Pope John Paul II during their meeting at the Vatican June 4, 2004. Pope John Paul told President Bush on Friday that Iraq had to regain sovereignty swiftly and deplored the abuse of Iraqi prisoners by U.S. troops.*

*President George W. Bush presents the Presidential Medal of Freedom, the highest U.S. civilian honor, to Pope John Paul II during his visit to the Vatican, June 4, 2004.*

*Above:* Pope John Paul looks at a baby during his Sunday Angelus prayer at his summer residence in Castelgandolfo, south of Rome, August 8, 2004.

*Right:* Pope John Paul II kneels in front of a crucifix during a beatification ceremony in St. Peter's Square at the Vatican October 3, 2004. Pope John Paul put five Catholics on the road to sainthood on Sunday, including Austria's last emperor, Karl I.

*Left Bottom:* Pope John Paul laughs with an infant at his weekly Sunday blessing at his summer residence in Castelgandolfo south of Rome August 1, 2004. In a clear and firm voice, he spoke of his coming trips to Lourdes, France in mid August and to the Italian city of Loreto in early September.

*Left Top:* President George W. Bush meets with Pope John Paul II at the Vatican June 4, 2004. Italians greeted American soldiers as liberators when they marched into Rome 60 years ago but President Bush faces deep anger on his visit on Friday over the actions of a new generation of U.S. soldiers in Iraq.

## Pope's Address to Bishops of New York State
## "Continue to Lead by Example"

VATICAN CITY, OCT. 8, 2004

Dear Brother Bishops,

1. It gives me great joy today to welcome you, the Pastors of the Church in New York, in the context of the continuing series of visits "ad limina Apostolorum" by the American Bishops. I greet you in the name of our Savior Jesus Christ, through whom we give thanks always to our heavenly Father "whose power now at work in us can do immeasurably more than we ask or imagine" (Ephesians 3:20).
In previous meetings with your fellow Bishops from the United States, attention has been focused on the sacred duty to sanctify and teach the People of God. With the group that preceded you I began to reflect on the great responsibility of governing the faithful. Let us continue today to examine this same "munus regendi," which must always be carried out in the spirit of the exhortation found in the Rite of Ordination of a Bishop: "The title of Bishop is one of service, not of honor, and therefore a Bishop should strive to benefit others rather than to lord it over them. Such is the precept of the Master" (Roman Pontifical, Rite of Ordination of a Bishop: Homily; cf. "Pastores Gregis," 43).

2. In your Particular Churches, you are called to act "in nomine Christi." Indeed, it is as vicars and ambassadors of Christ that you govern the portion of the flock entrusted to you (cf. "Lumen Gentium," 27). As shepherds, you "have the task of gathering together the family of the faithful and ...fostering charity and brotherly communion" ("Pastores Gregis," 5). Yet your immediate function as pastors cannot be isolated from your wider responsibility for the universal Church; as members of the College of Bishops, "cum et sub Petro," you in fact share in solicitude for the entire people of God, received through episcopal ordination and hierarchical communion (cf. "Lumen Gentium," 23). Moreover, while guaranteeing the communion of your Dioceses with the Church throughout the world, you also enable the universal Church to draw upon the life and the charisms of the local Church in a spiritual "exchange of gifts." Authentic "catholic" unity presupposes this mutual enrichment in the one Spirit.
Considered within a properly theological context, "power of governance" emerges as something more than mere "administration" or the exercise of organizational skills: it is a means for building up the Kingdom of God. I would encourage you, therefore, to continue to lead by example, in order to evangelize your flock for their own sanctification, thereby preparing them to share the Good News with others. Foster communion among them so as to equip them for the Church's mission. As you embrace lovingly the threefold "munera" entrusted to you, remember that your sacred responsibility to teach, sanctify and govern cannot be surrendered to anyone else: it is your personal vocation.

3. I am grateful for the deep affection which American Catholics have traditionally felt for the Successor of Peter, as well as their sensitivity and generosity to the needs of the Holy See and the universal Church. The Bishops of the United States have always shown a great love for the one in whom the Lord established "the lasting and visible source and foundation of the unity both of faith and of communion" ("Lumen Gentium," 18). Your abiding loyalty to the Roman Pontiff has led you to seek ways to strengthen the bond linking the Church in America with the Apostolic See. These devoted sentiments are a fruit of the hierarchical communion linking all members of the episcopal College with the Pope. At the same time, they constitute a great spiritual resource for the renewal of the Church in the United States. In encouraging your people to deepen their fidelity to the Magisterium and their union of mind and heart with the Successor of Peter, you offer them the inspirational leadership that is needed to carry them forward into the Third Millennium.

4. One of the fruits of the Second Vatican Council was a fresh understanding of episcopal collegiality. Among the ways in which this ecclesial vision is realized at the level of the local Church is through the activity of Episcopal Conferences. Bishops today can only fulfill their office fruitfully when they work harmoniously and closely with their fellow Bishops (cf. "Christus Dominus," 37, "Apostolos Suos," 15). For this reason, constant reflection is needed on the relationship between the Episcopal Conference and the individual Bishop.
My dear Brothers in the episcopate, I pray that you will work diligently with one another, in that spirit of cooperation and unanimity of heart that should always characterize the community of disciples (cf. Acts 4:32; John 13:35; Philippians 2:2). The Apostle's words apply in a special way to those charged with the salvation of souls: "I beg you, Brothers, in the name of our Lord Jesus Christ, to agree in what you say. Let there be no factions; rather, be united in mind and judgment" (1 Corinthians 1:10).
As Church leaders, you will realize that there can be no unity of praxis without an underlying consensus, and this, of course, can only be attained through frank dialogue

and informed discussions, based on sound theological and pastoral principles. Solutions to difficult questions emerge when they are thoroughly and honestly examined, under the guidance of the Holy Spirit. Spare no effort to ensure that the United States Conference of Catholic Bishops serves as an ever more effective means of strengthening your ecclesial communion and assisting you in shepherding your brothers and sisters in Christ.

5. Without prejudice, therefore, to the God-given authority of a Diocesan Bishop over his Particular Church, the Episcopal Conference should assist him in carrying out his mission in harmony with his brother Bishops. The structures and procedures of a Conference should never become unduly rigid; instead, through constant reassessment and reappraisal, they should be adapted to suit the changing needs of the Bishops. In order for a Conference to fulfill its proper function, care should be taken to ensure that the offices or commissions within a Conference strive "to be of help to the Bishops and not to substitute for them, and even less to create an intermediate structure between the Apostolic See and individual Bishops" ("Pastores Gregis," 63).

6. Brothers, I pray that at every opportunity you will be able to work together, so that the Gospel may be more effectively proclaimed throughout your country. I wish to express my appreciation for all that you have already accomplished together, particularly in your statements on life issues, education and peace. I invite you now to turn your attention to the many other pressing issues that directly affect the Church's mission and her spiritual integrity, for example the decline in Mass attendance and in recourse to the Sacrament of Reconciliation, the threats to marriage and the religious needs of immigrants. Let your voice be clearly heard, announcing the message of salvation in season and out of season (cf. 2 Timothy 4:1). Confidently preach the Good News so that all may be saved and come to the knowledge of the truth (cf. 1 Timothy 2:4).

7. As I conclude my remarks today, I make my own the words of Saint Paul: "Encourage one another. Live in harmony and peace, and the God of love and peace will be with you" (2 Corinthians 13:11). Entrusting you and your priests, deacons, religious and lay faithful to the intercession of Mary, Mother of America (cf. "Ecclesia in America," 76), I cordially impart my Apostolic Blessing as a pledge of grace and strength in her Son, our Lord Jesus Christ.

Pope John Paul II is covered by an umbrella as he arrives for his weekly Wednesday general audience in Saint Peter's Square at the Vatican October 27, 2004. The Pope prayed for the Iraqi people on Wednesday and said he shared the pain of kidnap victims and people hit by the blind barbarism of terrorism.

**Right:** Pope John Paul II waves to the faithful during his Angelus for All Saints Day in Saint Peter's Square at the Vatican. Pope John Paul II waves to the faithful during his Angelus for All Saints Day in Saint Peter's Square at the Vatican November 1, 2004. The Pope prayed for the victims of terrorism on Monday and said he felt spiritually close to the families.

*Above:* Pope John Paul II chats with Iraqi Prime Minister Ayad Allawi (L) during a private meeting in his library at the Vatican November 4, 2004.

*Left:* Pope John Paul II waves as he arrives to lead a special audience in Paul VI hall at the Vatican November 6, 2004.

*Right Top:* Pope John Paul II blesses Father Marcial Maciel during a special audience in Paul VI hall at the Vatican. Pope John Paul II blesses Father Marcial Maciel, founder of the Legion of Christ, during a special audience in Paul VI hall at the Vatican November 30, 2004.

*Right Bottom:* Pope John Paul II waves during his weekly Wednesday general audience in Paul VI hall at the Vatican December 1, 2004.

## Christmas Message of John Paul II
## "Everywhere Peace Is Needed"

DEC. 25, 2004

1. "Christus natus est nobis, venite, adoremus!" Christ is born for us: come, let us adore him! On this solemn day we come to you, tender Babe of Bethlehem. By your birth you have hidden your divinity in order to share our frail human nature. In the light of faith, we acknowledge you as true God, made man out of love for us. You alone are the Redeemer of mankind!

2. Before the crib where you lie helpless, let there be an end to the spread of violence in its many forms, the source of untold suffering; let there be an end to the numerous situations of unrest which risk degenerating into open conflict; let there arise a firm will to seek peaceful solutions, respectful of the legitimate aspirations of individuals and peoples.

3. Babe of Bethlehem, Prophet of peace, encourage attempts to promote dialogue and reconciliation, sustain the efforts to build peace, which hesitantly, yet not without hope, are being made to bring about a more tranquil present and future for so many of our brothers and sisters in the world. I think of Africa, of the tragedy of Darfur in Sudan, of Côte d'Ivoire and of the Great Lakes Region. With great apprehension I follow the situation in Iraq. And how can I fail to look with anxious concern, but also invincible confidence, towards that Land of which you are a son?

4. Everywhere peace is needed! You, Prince of true peace, help us to understand that the only way to build peace is to flee in horror from evil, and to pursue goodness with courage and perseverance. Men and women of good will, of every people on the earth, come with trust to the crib of the Savior! "He who bestows the Kingdom of heaven does not take away human kingdoms" (cf. Hymn for Vespers of Epiphany). Hasten to meet him; he comes to teach us the way of truth, peace and love.

**Right:** *Pope John Paul II waves as he passes in front of the traditional Crib in St Peter's square at the end of the Te Deum prayer in St Peter's Basilica at the Vatican, December 31, 2004. The pontiff ended the year with words of thanks for the last 12 months and a hopeful eye toward 2005, in his traditional New Year's Eve address to Roman churchgoers.*

**Below:** *Pope John Paul II looks at an unidentified child during his weekly general audience at the Vatican December 29, 2004. The Pope appealed on Wednesday to the world to seize the Christmas spirit and generously help survivors of southern Asia's devastating tsumani, while praising the swift response so far.*

## State of the World, According to John Paul II

### Address to the Diplomatic Corps Accredited to the Holy See

JAN. 10, 2005

*Your Excellencies, Ladies and Gentlemen,*

*1. The quiet joy which marks this season when the Church relives the mystery of the birth of Emmanuel and the mystery of his humble family in Nazareth, is very much a part of this, my yearly meeting with you, the distinguished Ambassadors and members of the diplomatic corps accredited to the Holy See. In gathering here today, you in a certain way make visible the great family of the Nations.*

*This joy-filled and long-awaited meeting has opened with the message of good wishes, respect and appreciation for my universal concern on the part of your Dean, Professor Giovanni Galassi, Ambassador of San Marino. I am grateful for his kind words and I reciprocate with good wishes of peace and joy for all of you and your beloved families, and of peace and prosperity for the countries you represent.*

*I offer a particularly cordial word of welcome and good wishes to the thirty-seven Ambassadors who began their mission at the See of Peter in the past year, and to the members of their families.*

*2. These sentiments of joy are overshadowed, unfortunately, by the enormous catastrophe which on 26 December struck different countries of Southeast Asia and as far as the coasts of East Africa. It made for a painful ending of the year just past: a year troubled also by other natural calamities, such as the devastating cyclones in the Indian Ocean and the Antilles, and the plague of locusts which desolated vast regions of Northwest Africa. Other tragedies also cast a shadow on 2004, like the acts of barbarous terrorism which caused bloodshed in Iraq and other countries of the world, the savage attack in Madrid, the terrorist massacre in Beslan, the inhuman acts of violence inflicted on the people of Darfur, the atrocities perpetrated in the Great Lakes region of Africa.*

*These events have caused great anguish and distress, and we would feel a tragic concern for the future of humanity, were it not for the fact that from the cradle of Bethlehem there comes to us a message, both divine and human, of life and more certain hope: in Jesus Christ, who comes into the world as the brother of every man and woman and takes his place at our side, it is God himself who asks us not to yield to discouragement, but to overcome every difficulty, however great it may be, by strengthening the common bonds of our humanity and by making them prevail over all other considerations.*

*3. Your presence here, as representatives of almost all the peoples of the earth, immediately sets before our eyes the great tableau of humanity with its grave and troubling problems and its great and undampened hopes. The Catholic Church, because of her universal nature, is always directly engaged in the great causes for which the men and women of our age struggle and hope. She considers herself a stranger to no people, since wherever there are Christians, the whole body of the Church is called into play; indeed, wherever there is any one individual, we sense a bond of brotherhood. In her presence and her concern for the future of men and women everywhere, the Holy See knows that it can count on Your Excellencies to offer an important service, since it is precisely the mission of diplomats to transcend borders and to bring peoples and governments together in the desire to cooperate harmoniously, in scrupulous respect for each other's competencies, but at the same time in the quest for a higher common good.*

*4. In my Message for this year's World Day of Peace, I called the attention of the Catholic faithful and of all men and women of good will to the exhortation of the Apostle Paul: "Do not be overcome by evil, but overcome evil with good": "vince in bono malum" (Romans 12:21). There is a profound truth underlying these words: In the moral and social sphere, evil takes on the countenance of selfishness and hatred, which is negativity; it can only be overcome by love, which has the positivity of generous and disinterested giving, even to the point of self-sacrifice. This is the heart of the mystery of Christ's birth: To save humanity from the selfishness of sin and its corollary of death, God himself lovingly enters, in Christ, into the fullness of life, into human history, thus raising humanity to the horizon of an even greater life.*

*This is the message -- "overcome evil with good" -- which I would like to address today to your Excellencies, and through you to the beloved peoples whom you represent and to your Governments. This message also has a specific application to international relations,* and it can be a guide to all in meeting the great challenges facing humanity today. Here I would like to point out some of the more significant ones:

5. The first is the challenge of life. Life is the first gift which God has given us, it is the first resource which man can enjoy. The Church is called to proclaim "the Gospel of Life." And the State has as its primary task precisely the safeguarding and promotion of human life.

The challenge to life has grown in scale and urgency in recent years. It has involved particularly the beginning of human life, when human beings are at their weakest and most in need of protection. Conflicting views have been put forward regarding abortion, assisted procreation, the use of human embryonic stem cells for scientific research, and cloning. The Church's position, supported by reason and science, is clear: The human embryo is a subject identical to the human being which will be born at the term of its development. Consequently whatever violates the integrity and the dignity of the embryo is ethically inadmissible. Similarly, any form of scientific research which treats the embryo merely as a laboratory specimen is unworthy of man. Scientific research in the field of genetics needs to be encouraged and promoted, but, like every other human activity, it can never be exempt from moral imperatives; research using adult stem cells, moreover, offers the promise of considerable success.

The challenge to life has also emerged with regard to the very sanctuary of life: the family. Today the family is often threatened by social and cultural pressures which tend to undermine its stability; but in some countries the family is also threatened by legislation which -- at times directly -- challenge its natural structure, which is and must necessarily be that of a union between a man and a woman founded on marriage. The family, as a fruitful source of life and a fundamental and irreplaceable condition for the happiness of the individual spouses, for the raising of children and for the well-being of society, and indeed for the material prosperity of the nation, must never be undermined by laws based on a narrow and unnatural vision of man. There needs to prevail a just, pure and elevated understanding of human love, which finds in the family its primordial and exemplary expression. "Vince in bono malum."

6. The second challenge is that of food. This world, made wondrously fruitful by its Creator, possesses a sufficient quantity and variety of food for all its inhabitants, now and in the future. Yet the statistics on world hunger are dramatic: hundreds of millions of human beings are suffering from grave malnutrition, and each year millions of children die of hunger or its effects.

In fact, the alarm has been raised for some time now, and the leading international organizations have set important targets, at least for reducing the emergency. Concrete proposals have also been put forward, such as those discussed at the Meeting in New York on hunger and poverty held on 20 September 2004. I had asked Cardinal Angelo Sodano, Secretary of State, to represent me at that meeting, as a way of demonstrating the Church's great interest in this dramatic problem. Many non-governmental associations have also been generously committed to providing assistance. Yet all this is not enough. An adequate response to this need, which is growing in scale and urgency, calls for a vast moral mobilization of public opinion; the same applies all the more to political leaders, especially in those countries enjoying a sufficient or even prosperous standard of living.

In this regard, I would like to recall an important principle of the Church's social teaching, to which I once again made reference in my Message for this year's World Day of Peace and included in the recently-published Compendium of the Social Doctrine of the Church: the principle of the universal destination of the earth's goods. While this principle cannot be used to justify collectivist forms of economic policy, it should serve to advance a radical commitment to justice and a more attentive and determined display of solidarity. This is the good which can overcome the evil of hunger and unjust poverty. "Vince in bono malum."

7. There is also the challenge of peace. As a supreme good and the condition for attaining many other essential goods, peace is the dream of every generation. Yet how many wars and armed conflicts continue to take place -- between States, ethnic groups, peoples and groups living in the same territory. From one end of the world to the other, they are claiming countless innocent victims and spawning so many other evils! Our thoughts naturally turn to different countries in the Middle East, Africa, Asia and Latin America, where recourse to arms and violence has not only led to incalculable material damage, but also fomented hatred and increased the causes of tension, thereby adding to the difficulty of finding and implementing solutions capable of reconciling the legitimate interests of all the parties involved. In addition to these tragic evils there is the brutal, inhuman phenomenon of terrorism, a scourge which has taken on a global dimension unknown to previous generations.

How can the great challenge of building peace overcome such evils? As diplomats, you are men and women of peace by profession but also by personal vocation. You know the nature and extent of the means which the international community has at its disposal for keeping or restoring peace. Like my venerable predecessors, I have spoken out countless times, in public statements -- especially in my annual Message for the World Day of Peace -- and through the Holy See's diplomatic activity, and I shall continue to do so, pointing out the paths to peace and urging that they be followed with courage and patience. The arrogance of power must be countered with reason, force with dialogue,

pointed weapons with outstretched hands, evil with good.

Many indeed are the men and women who are working towards this goal with courage and perseverance, and there are some encouraging signs that the great challenge of building peace can be met. In Africa, for instance, despite serious relapses into disagreements which appeared to have been resolved, there is a growing common will to resolve and prevent conflicts through a fuller cooperation between the great international organizations and continental groupings, like the African Union: examples of this were had in the meeting of the United Nations Security Council in Nairobi last November to discuss the humanitarian emergency in Darfur and the situation in Somalia, and in the international Conference on the Great Lakes region. In the Middle East, the land so dear and sacred to believers in the God of Abraham, armed confrontation appears to be decreasing, with the hope of a political breakthrough in the direction of dialogue and negotiation. Certainly an outstanding example of the possibility of peace can be seen in Europe: Nations which were once fierce enemies locked in deadly wars are now members of the European Union, which during the past year aimed at further consolidation through the constitutional Treaty of Rome, while at the same time showing an openness to admitting other States willing to accept the requirements of membership.

Bringing about an authentic and lasting peace in this violence-filled world calls for a power of good that does not shrink before difficulties. It is a power that human beings on their own cannot obtain or preserve: It is a gift from God. Christ came to bring this gift to mankind, as the angels sang above the manger in Bethlehem: "peace among men with whom he is pleased" (Luke 2:14). God loves mankind, and he wants peace for all men and women. We are asked to be active instruments of that peace, and to overcome evil with good. "Vince in bono malum."

8. There is another challenge that I wish to mention: the challenge of freedom. All of you know how important this is to me, especially because of the history of my native people, yet it is also important to each of you. In your service as diplomats you are rightly concerned to protect the freedom of the peoples you represent, and you are diligent in defending that freedom. Yet freedom is first and foremost a right of each individual. As the Universal Declaration of Human Rights fittingly states in Article 1 - "all human beings are born free and equal in dignity and rights." Article 3 goes on to state that "everyone has the right to life, liberty and security of person." Certainly the freedom of States is also sacred; they need to be free, above all so that they can carry out adequately their fundamental duty of safeguarding both the life and the freedom of their citizens in all their legitimate manifestations.

Freedom is a great good, because only by freedom can human beings find fulfillment in a manner befitting their nature. Freedom is like light: It enables one to choose responsibly his proper goals and the right means of achieving them. At the very heart of human freedom is the right to religious freedom, since it deals with man's most fundamental relationship: his relationship with God. Religious freedom is expressly guaranteed in the Universal Declaration of Human Rights (cf. Article 18). It was also the subject - as all of you are well aware - of a solemn Declaration of the Second Vatican Ecumenical Council, one which began with the significant words "Dignitatis Humanae."

In many States, freedom of religion is a right which is not yet sufficiently or adequately recognized. Yet the yearning for freedom of religion cannot be suppressed: As long as human beings are alive, it will always be present and pressing. Consequently I repeat today an appeal which the Church has already made on numerous occasions: "It is necessary that religious freedom be everywhere provided with an effective constitutional guarantee, and that respect be shown for the high duty and right of man freely to lead his religious life in society" ("Dignitatis Humanae," 15).

There need be no fear that legitimate religious freedom would limit other freedoms or be injurious to the life of civil society. On the contrary: together with religious freedom, all other freedoms develop and thrive, inasmuch as freedom is an indivisible good, the prerogative of the human person and his dignity. Neither should there be a fear that religious freedom, once granted to the Catholic Church, would intrude upon the realm of political freedom and the competencies proper to the State: The Church is able carefully to distinguish, as she must, what belongs to Caesar from what belongs to God (cf. Matthew 22:21). She actively cooperates in promoting the common good of society, inasmuch as she repudiates falsehood and educates to truth, she condemns hatred and contempt, and she calls for a spirit of brotherhood; always and everywhere she encourages -- as history clearly shows -- works of charity, science and the arts. She asks only for freedom, so that she can effectively cooperate with all public and private institutions concerned with the good of mankind. True freedom always aims at overcoming evil with good. "Vince in bono malum."

Your Excellencies, in the year now beginning I am certain that, as you carry out your lofty mandate, you will continue to accompany the Holy See in its daily efforts to meet, in accordance with its specific responsibilities, the abovementioned challenges which affect all humanity. Jesus Christ, whose birth we have celebrated in these days, was foretold by the Prophet as Admirabilis Consiliarius, Princeps Pacis, "Wonderful Counselor, Prince of Peace" (Isaiah 9:5). May the light of his word, his spirit of justice and brotherhood, and the gift of his peace, so needed and so desired, a peace which he offers to all, shine upon your lives, your beloved families and your dear ones, upon your noble countries and upon all humanity.

**Pope's Message to Peoples Affected by Tsunami**
**"May This Catastrophe Lead to a Future of Greater Generosity"**

JAN. 30, 2005

*Pope John Paul II poses with a group of U.S. priests during his weekly Wednesday general audience at the Vatican, January 19, 2005.*

To the Most Reverend Paul Josef Cordes
President of the Pontifical Council "Cor Unum"

The enormous devastation and loss of life associated with the recent earthquake and tidal wave in Southeast Asia has been followed by a remarkable outpouring of sympathy throughout the world, together with a massive mobilization of humanitarian aid. I am deeply grateful for the efforts of the Pontifical Council "Cor Unum" and numerous international Catholic charitable agencies to contribute to the relief of the peoples struck by this immense natural disaster.

As you depart for a visit to that region, I would ask you to convey the assurance of my concern and my closeness in prayer to all affected by the tragedy and its aftermath. In particular, I join my fellow Catholics and all believers in commending the victims of this terrible calamity to the infinite mercy of Almighty God and in imploring divine consolation upon the injured, the grieving and the homeless.

I pray that the solidarity shown by our brothers and sisters throughout the world will prove a source of encouragement, perseverance and hope to everyone in the great work of rebuilding that lies ahead. I likewise urge the followers of the different religions to work together in offering comfort and assistance to those in need. May this catastrophe lead, by God's grace, to a future of greater generosity, cooperation and unity in the service of the common good on the part of individuals, peoples and nations.

As I hold up to all the light of the Gospel, I express my fervent hope that the Christian community will be led to a deepened trust in God's mysterious providence and an ever closer union to the Lord Jesus in the mystery of his suffering and resurrection.

Upon the civil authorities and all engaged in the relief efforts I invoke the divine gifts of wisdom and strength. To you, dear Brother, and to all the clergy, religious and lay faithful of the communities you will visit, I cordially impart my Apostolic Blessing as a pledge of grace and peace in the Lord.

**Ioannes Paulus PP. II**
**Karol Wojtyla**
**16.X.1978 - 2.IV.2005**

APRIL 2, 2005

*The Holy Father died at 9:37 (2:37 EST) this evening in his private apartment.*

*At 8 p.m. the celebration of Mass for Divine Mercy Sunday began in the Holy Father's room, presided by Archbishop Stanislaw Dziwisz, with the participation of Cardinal Marian Jaworski, of Archbishop Stanislaw Rylko and of Monsignor Mieczyslaw Mokrzycki.*
*During the course of the Mass, the Viaticum was administered to the Holy Father and, once again, the Sacrament of Anointing of the Sick.*
*The Holy Father's final hours were marked by the uninterrupted prayer of all those who were assisting him in his pious death, and by the choral participation in prayer of the thousands of faithful who, for many hours, had been gathered in St. Peter's Square.*

*Present at the moment of the death of John Paul II were: his two personal secretaries, Archbishop Stanislaw Dziwisz and Monsignor Mieczyslaw Mokrzycki, Cardinal Marian Jaworski, Archbishop Stanislaw Rylko, Father Tadeusz Styczen, the three nuns, Handmaidens of the Sacred Heart of Jesus, who assist in the Holy Father's apartment, guided by the Superior Sister Tobiana Sobódka, and the Pope's personal physician Dr. Renato Buzzonetti, with the two doctors on call, Dr. Alessandro Barelli and Dr. Ciro D'Allo, and the two nurses on call.*

*Immediately afterwards the secretary of state, Cardinal Angelo Sodano arrived, as did the chamberlain of Holy Roman Church, Cardinal Eduardo Martinez Somalo, Archbishop Leonardo Sandri, substitute of the Secretariat of State, and Archbishop Paolo Sardi, vice-chamberlain of Holy Roman Church.*

*Thereafter, Cardinal Joseph Ratzinger, dean of the College of Cardinals, and Cardinal Jozef Tomko also arrived.*

*Tomorrow, Divine Mercy Sunday, at 10.30 a.m., a Mass for the repose of the soul of the Holy Father will be celebrated in St. Peter's Square, presided over by Cardinal Angelo Sodano.*

*At 12 noon, the Marian prayer of Easter time, the Regina Coeli, will be recited. The body of the late pontiff is expected to be brought to the Vatican Basilica no earlier than Monday afternoon.*
*The first General Congregation of Cardinals will be held at 10 a.m. on Monday, April 4 in the Bologna Hall of the Apostolic Palace.*

**Below:** *Polish faithful pray during a special mass for the late Pope John Paul II at Pilsudski Square in Warsaw April 3, 2005. More than 100,000 worshippers packed the central square in the capital Warsaw, while 60,000 gathered in Krakow.*

*Faithful gather at Saint Peter's Square for a solemn mass led by Italian Cardinal Angelo Sodano to pay respect to the death of Pope John Paul II at the Vatican April 3, 2005. The world mourned the late Pope on Sunday and thousands of grieving pilgrims converged on Rome to pay homage to the Pope.*

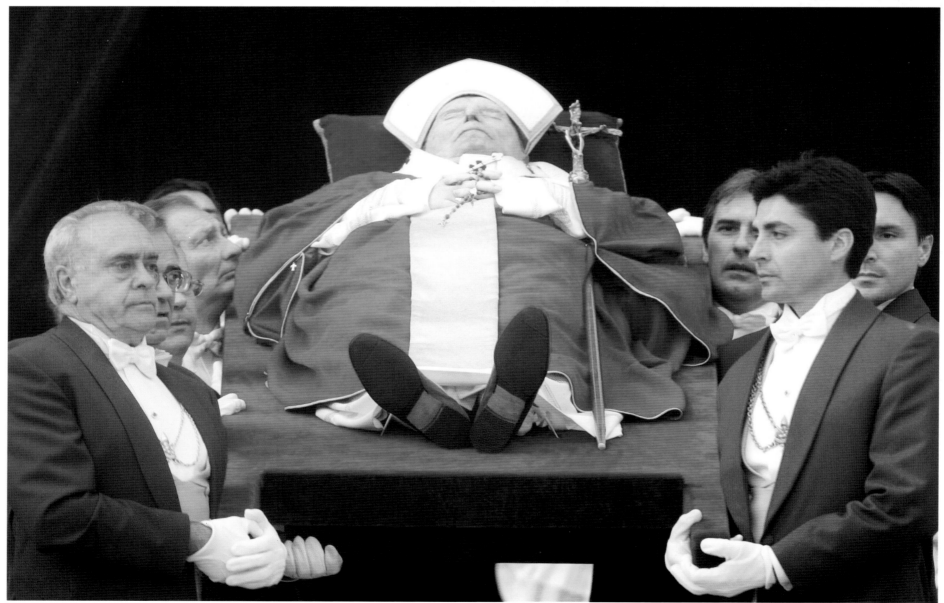

**Left Top:** *Britain's Prince Charles (L) and Camilla Parker-Bowles attend a service in memory of Pope John Paul II at London's Westminster Cathedral April 4, 2005.*

**Left Bottom:** *Pall bearers carry the body of the late Pope John Paul II from Saint Peter's Square enroute to the Basilica at the Vatican April 4, 2005.*

**Above:** *Mourners pour into the Vatican's St. Peter's Basilica past the crimson-robed body of Pope John Paul II. Mourners pour into the Vatican's St. Peter's Basilica past the crimson-robed body of Pope John Paul II April 5, 2005.*

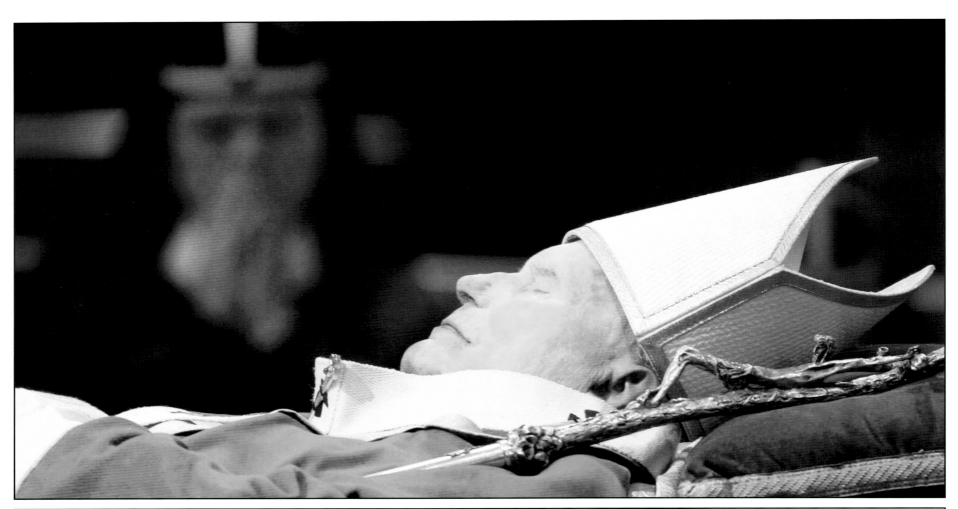

**Far Left Top:** *The body of Pope John Paul II lies in state in Saint Peter's Basilica at the Vatican April 5, 2005. Up to two million people are expected for the funeral on Friday as well as almost 200 world leaders in an unprecedented salute for a pontiff who helped bring down the Iron Curtain and stamped an uncompromising orthodoxy on his own faith.*

**Far Left Bottom:** *Monaco's Prince Albert (L), Princess Caroline of Hanover (R) and her daughter Charlotte (2nd L) arrive for a memorial mass for Pope John Paul II at Monaco cathedral April 5, 2005.*

**Left:** *Cardinal Renato Martino kneels and prays under the statue of Saint Peter as the late Pope John Paul II lies in state in St. Peter's Basilica at the Vatican April 5, 2005.*

**Below:** *A young boy lights a candle on the market square near Mariacki church in Krakow April 7, 2005.*

**Above:** *A general view shows a packed Saint Peter's Square as pilgrims and dignitaries wait for the funeral of Pope John Paul II at the Vatican April 8, 2005.*

**Left:** *Nuns hold rosaries near Saint Peter's Square as while they await the start of the funeral mass for Pope John Paul II April 8, 2005. Some 200 heads of state, heads of government and royalty will gather here today to attend the late pontiff's funeral.*

**Far Left:** *People gather for a mass and the live transmission of the funeral of the late Pope John Paul II at Blonie public meadows in Krakow, April 8, 2005.*

**Left Top:** *A simple wooden coffin with the remains of the late Pope John Paul II is put in place at the start of his funeral mass in St. Peter's Square at the Vatican April 8, 2005.*

**Left Bottom:** *Priests arrive for the funeral of Pope John Paul II in the Vatican's St. Peter's Square April 8, 2005.*

**Below:** *Roman Catholic priests attend the funeral of Pope John Paul II in the Vatican's St. Peter's Square April 8, 2005.*

*Left Top:* Roman Catholic cardinals attend the funeral of Pope John Paul II in the Vatican's St. Peter's Square.

*Left Bottom:* Mourners hold a banner that reads 'Sainthood immediately', during a funeral Mass for Pope John Paul II in the Vatican's St Peter's Square April 8, 2005.

*Right:* Nuns rest near Saint Peter's Square as they await the start of the funeral mass for Pope John Paul II April 8, 2005.

*Below:* Mourners fill St. Peter's Square during the funeral mass for Pope John Paul II at the Vatican April 8, 2005.

*U.S. President George W. Bush (2nd R) is greeted by Bishop James Harvey (L) as he arrives to attend the funeral of Pope John Paul II in the Vatican's St. Peter's square April 8, 2005.*

**Left:** *Grand Duke Henri (R) and Grand Duchess Maria Teresa of Luxembourg attend the funeral of Pope John Paul II at the Vatican's St. Peter's square April 8, 2005.*

*Bishop Piero Marini (L) puts the Book of the Gospel on the coffin of the late Pope John Paul II for his funeral in the Vatican's St. Peter's Basilica April 8, 2005.*

*Iran's President Mohammad Khatami (centre row R), Syria's President Bashar al-Assad (rear 3rd L) and Israel's President Moshe Katsav (centre row L) stand amongst other dignitaries during the funeral of Pope John Paul II in St. Peter's Square at the Vatican.*

**Above:** *Monarchs, heads of state and other dignitaries attend the funeral of Pope John Paul II in the Vatican's St. Peter's square April 8, 2005. A simple cypress coffin bearing Pope John Paul's body was carried out of St. Peter's Basilica on Friday as a funeral mass started for the poor and powerful of the earth to say their last goodbye.*

**Below:** *France's President Jacques Chirac (L) and his wife Bernadette (2nd L), U.S. first lady Laura Bush (2nd R) and U.S. President George W. Bush (R) sit behind Spain's King Juan Carlos (front R) and Queen Sofia (front L)*

Left Top: *Jordan's King Abdullah (R) and his wife Queen Rania (L) sit in St. Peter's Square at the start of the funeral mass for the late Pope John Paul II at the Vatican April 8, 2005.*

Left Bottom: *Polish President Aleksander Kwasniewski (R) and his wife Jolanta (2nd R) sit with Italian President Carlo Azeglio Ciampi (L) and his wife Franca (2nd L) at the start of the funeral mass for Pope John Paul II at the Vatican.*

Above: *Germany's Chancellor Gerhard Schroeder (C) and Foreign Minister Joschka Fischer (R) are surrounded by other dignitaries during the funeral of the late Pope John Paul II.*

Right: *U.N. Secretary-General Kofi Annan (L), British Prime Minister Tony Blair (C) and Britain's Prince Charles mingle with other guests at the funeral for the late Pope John Paul II in St. Peter's Square at the Vatican April 8, 2005.*

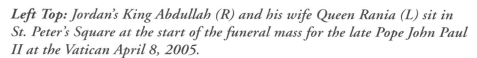

*Left: Pallbearers carry the coffin of Pope John Paul II into the Vatican's St. Peter's Basilica after his funeral Mass April 8, 2005.*

*Below: Italian Archbishop Piero Marini puts a small bag of commemorative medals in Pope John Paul II's coffin before closing it for burial in the grottos beneath the Vatican's St. Peter's Basilica April 8, 2005.*

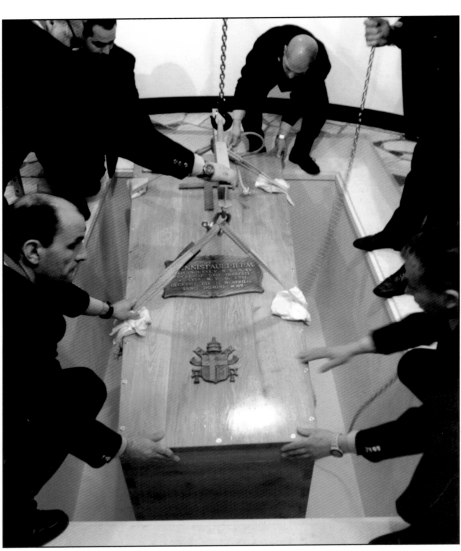

Pope John Paul II's coffin is lowered into the crypt below the Vatican's St. Peter's Basilica after his funeral Mass April 8, 2005.

The crypt of late Pope John Paul II lies in the grotto of the Vatican's St. Peter's Basilica April 9, 2005.